SLAVERY IN THE AMERICAS

The Slave Trade

Matthew Kachur

Philip Schwarz, Ph.D., *General Editor*

CHELSEA HOUSE
PUBLISHERS
An imprint of Infobase Publishing

Slavery in the Americas: *The Slave Trade*

Chelsea House
An imprint of Infobase Publishing
132 West 31st Street
New York NY 10001

Library of Congress Cataloging-in-Publication Data
Kachur, Matthew, 1960–
    The slave trade / Matthew Kachur.
           p. cm. — (Slavery in the Americas)
    Includes bibliographical references and index.
    ISBN 0-8160-6134-3
    1. Slave trade—United States—History—Juvenile literature. 2. Slave trade—North America—History—Juvenile literature. 3. Slavery—United States—History—Juvenile literature. I. Title. II. Series.
    E442.K33 2006
    306.3'620973—dc22
                                  2005031709

Chelsea House books are available at special discounts when purchased in bulk quantities for businesses, associations, institutions, or sales promotions. Please call our Special Sales Department in New York at (212) 967-8800 or (800) 322-8755.

You can find Chelsea House on the World Wide Web at http://www.chelseahouse.com

Cover design by Smart Graphics
A Creative Media Applications Production
Interior design: Fabia Wargin & Luís Leon
Editor: Matt Levine
Copy editor: Laurie Lieb
Proofreader: Tania Bissell
Photo researcher: Jennifer Bright

Photo credits
New York Public Library, Astor, Lenox and Tilden Foundations pages: title page, 14, 17, 20, 27, 44, 47, 49, 51, 77, 85, 87, 102; The Granger Collection pages: 5, 57, 73, 95, 96, 99; Associated Press page: 10; Library of Congress pages: 25, 39, 68, 82, 100; The Bridgeman Art Library pages: 37, 75; Colonial Williamsburg Foundation page: 41; North Wind Picture Archives pages: 63, 92

Printed in the United States of America

VB PKG 10 9 8 7 6 5 4 3 2 1

This book is printed on acid-free paper.

PREVIOUS PAGE:

Slaves captured in Africa are led to the coast, where they will be loaded on a ship and brought to the Americas.

Contents

Preface to the Series

Philip Schwarz, Ph.D., *General Editor*

In order to understand American history, it is essential to know that for nearly two centuries, Americans in the 13 colonies and then in the United States bought imported Africans and kept them and their descendants in bondage. In his second inaugural address in March 1865, President Abraham Lincoln mentioned the "250 years of unrequited toil" that slaves had endured in America. Slavery lasted so long and controlled so many people's lives that it may seem impossible to comprehend the phenomenon and to know the people involved. Yet it is extremely difficult to grasp many aspects of life in today's United States without learning about slavery's role in the lives and development of the American people.

Slavery probably existed before history began to be recorded, but the first known dates of slavery are about 1600 B.C. in Greece and as early as 2700 B.C. in Mesopotamia (present-day Iraq). Although there are institutions that resemble slavery in some modern societies, slavery in its actual sense is illegal everywhere. Yet historical slavery still affects today's free societies.

Numerous ancient and modern slave societies were based on chattel slavery—the legal ownership of human beings, not just their labor. The Bible's Old and New Testaments, as well as other ancient historical documents, describe enslaved people. Throughout history, there were slaves in African, Middle Eastern, South Asian, and East Asian societies, as well as in the Americas—and of course, there were slaves in European countries. (One origin of the word *slave* is the medieval Latin *sclavus*, which not only means "slave" but also "Slav." The Slavs were people of eastern Europe who were conquered in the 800s and often sold as slaves.)

This drawing shows slaves carrying their master in a garden in ancient Rome. Slaves were a part of many societies from ancient times until the mid-1800s.

People found as many excuses or justifications for enslaving other people as there were slaveholding societies. Members of one ethnic group claimed that cultural differences justified enslaving people of another group. People with long histories of conflict with other groups might conclude that those other people were inferior in some cultural way. Citizens of ancient Greece and Rome, among others, claimed they could hold other people in bondage because these people were "barbarians" or prisoners of war. Racism played a major part in European decisions to enslave Africans. European colonists in the Americas commonly argued that Africans and their descendants were naturally inferior to Europeans, so it was morally acceptable to enslave them.

New World slavery deeply affected both Africa and the Americas. African society changed dramatically when the Atlantic slave trade began to carry so many Africans away. Some African societies were weakened by the regular buying or kidnapping of valued community members.

Western Hemisphere societies also underwent extraordinary changes when slavery of Africans was established there. Black slavery in North America was part of society from the earliest colonial settlements until the end of the U.S. Civil War. Many people consider the sale of about 20 Africans in Jamestown, Virginia, in 1619 the beginning of African slavery in what became the United States. American Indians and, later, Africans also were enslaved in Spanish colonies such as today's Florida and California and the islands of the Caribbean.

In early to mid-17th-century colonial North America, slavery developed slowly, beginning in Maryland and Virginia and spreading to the Carolinas in the 1670s. Southern colonists originally relied on white European servants. However, many of these servants had signed contracts to work only for a certain number of years, often to pay for their passage to North America. They became free when these contracts expired. Other servants rebelled or escaped. When fewer Europeans were available as servants, the servants' prices rose. The colonists hoped to find a more easily controlled and cheaper labor supply. European slave traders captured and imported more Africans, and slave prices dropped.

Soon, American plantations became strong markets for enslaved Africans. Tobacco plantation owners in the colonies around Chesapeake Bay—Maryland, Virginia, and North Carolina—and rice growers in South Carolina pressured slave traders to supply more slaves. In time, more and more slaves were kidnapped from their homes in Africa and taken to the colonies in chains to cultivate crops on the growing number of Southern plantations. Slaves were also taken to the Northern colonies to be farm workers, household servants, and artisans. In 1790, the U.S. enslaved population was less than 700,000. By 1860, it had risen to 3,953,750.

Similar circumstances transformed the Caribbean and South American societies and economies into plantation economies. There was a high demand for sugar in Europe, so British, French, Spanish, Portuguese, and other European colonists tried to fill that need. Brazil, a Portuguese colony, also became a thriving coffee-producing region. As the sugar and coffee planters became successful, they increased the size of their plantations and therefore needed more slaves to do the work. By 1790, Brazil was the largest American colonial slave society—that is, a society whose economy and social structure were grounded in slavery. Some 1,442,800 enslaved people lived in Brazil in 1790—twice the number that lived in the United States. Brazil's slave population grew slowly, however; in 1860, it was still only about 1,715,000. However, South American slaves were forced to work extremely hard in the tropical heat. The death rate of Caribbean and South American plantation workers was much higher than that of the North American slaves. Occasionally, a North American slave owner would threaten to sell unruly slaves to the West Indies or South America. Enslaved people took the threat seriously because the West Indies' bad reputation was widespread.

It is estimated that at least 11.8 million people were captured and shipped from Africa to the Americas. Many died during the slave ship voyage across the Atlantic Ocean. About 10 million survived and were sold in the Americas from 1519 to 1867. Nearly one-third of those people went to Brazil, while only about 3.8 percent (391,000) came to North America.

If the 1619 "first Africans" were slaves—the record is not completely clear—then there was a massive increase of the enslaved North American population from 20 or so people to nearly 4 million. In 1860, known descendants of Africans, both enslaved and free, numbered approximately 4.5 million, or about 14 percent of the U.S. population.

Slaveholders thought several numbers best measured their social, political, and economic status. These were the number of human beings they owned, the money and labor value of those people, and the proportion of slaveholders' total investment in human beings. By the 1800s, Southern slaveholders usually held two-thirds of their worth in human property. The largest slave owners were normally the wealthiest people in their area. For example, one Virginian colonist, Robert "King" Carter, who died in 1733, owned 734 slaves.

Consider what it took for slavery to begin in North America and to last all the way to 1865 in the South. This historical phenomenon did not "just occur." Both slave owning and enslaved people made many decisions concerning enslavement.

Should people hold other people in lifetime bondage? Could Africans be imported without damaging American colonial societies? Should colonists give up slavery? It took many years before Americans reached consensus on these subjects. White people's consensus in the North eventually led to the outlawing of slavery there. The Southern white consensus was clearly proslavery. Enslaved peoples had to make different decisions. Should slaves resist slavery individually or in groups? Should they raise families when their children were likely to live and die in bondage? Over the two centuries in which North American slavery existed, enslaved people changed their opinions concerning these questions.

Some white colonists initially tried to own Indian slaves. However, because the Indians knew the local environment, they could escape somewhat easily, especially because their free relatives and friends would try to protect them. Also, European diseases simply killed many of these Indians. Once European enslavement of American Indians died out in the 18th century, Africans and their African-American descendants were the only slaves in America. The Africans and their children were people with a history. They represented numerous African societies from West Africa to Madagascar in the western Indian Ocean. They endured and survived, creating their own American history.

When Africans began families in North America, they created a new genealogy and new traditions regarding how to survive as slaves. They agonized over such matters as violent, or even group, resistance—if it was unlikely to succeed, why try? By the 1800s, they endured family losses to the interstate slave trade. Black families suffered new separations that often were as wrenching as those caused by the journey from Africa. Large numbers of black Americans were forced to move from the older (Upper South) states to the newer (Deep South) territories and states. They were often ripped from their families and everything they knew and forced to live and work in faraway places.

This undated illustration of pre–Civil War life depicts African men being held in slave pens in Washington, D.C., about 1850.

There was only so much that African-American people could do to resist enslavement once it became well established in America. People sometimes ask why slaves did not try to end their bondage by revolting. Some did, but they rarely succeeded in freeing themselves. Most individual "revolts"—more accurately termed resistance—were very localized and were more likely to succeed than large-scale revolts. A man or woman might refuse to do what owners wanted, take the punishment, and find another way to resist. Some were so effective in day-to-day resistance that they can be called successful. Others failed and then decided that they had to try to find ways to survive slavery and enjoy some aspects of life. Those who escaped as "fugitives," temporarily or permanently, were the most successful resisters. Frederick Douglass and Harriet Tubman are the most famous escapees. Solomon Northup was unique: He was born free, then kidnapped and sold into slavery. Northup escaped and published his story.

Although inhumane and designed to benefit slave owners, slavery was a very "human" institution. That is, slaveholders and enslaved people interacted in many different ways. The stories of individuals reveal this frequently complex human interaction.

There were, for example, in all the Southern states, free African Americans who became slave owners. They protected their own family members from slavery, but owned other human beings for profit. One such black slave owner, William Johnson of Mississippi, controlled his human property using the same techniques, both mild and harsh, as did white slave owners. Robert Lumpkin, a slave trader from Richmond, Virginia, sold thousands of human beings to

Deep South buyers. Yet Lumpkin had a formerly enslaved wife to whom he willed all his Virginia, Alabama, and Pennsylvania property in 1866. Lumpkin sent their children to Massachusetts and Pennsylvania for their education and protection. He also freed other slaves before 1865. How could men such as these justify protecting their own families, but at the same time separating so many other families?

The Thirteenth Amendment ended slavery in the United States. However, former slaves were often kept from owning property and did not share the same rights as white Americans. Racist laws and practices kept the status of black Americans low. Even though slavery ended well over a century ago, the descendants of slave owners and of slaves are still generally on markedly different economic levels from each other.

The Civil War and Reconstruction created massive upheaval in Southern slave and free black communities. In addition, slave owners were often devastated. African Americans were "free at last," but their freedom was not guaranteed. A century passed before their legal rights were effectively protected and their political participation expanded. The Reverend Martin Luther King's "I have a dream" speech placed the struggle in historical context: He said he had a dream that "the sons of former slaves and the sons of former slave owners will be able to sit down together at the table of brotherhood." (Today, he would surely mention daughters as well.) The weight of history had already delayed that dream's coming to pass and can still do so. Knowing the history of slavery and emancipation will help fulfill the dream.

Introduction

From 1400 to 1900, the transatlantic slave trade was responsible for taking millions of Africans from their homes and families and bringing them to the Americas as slaves.

A slave is a person who is owned by someone else and is forced to work for that person. He or she is completely under the control of that person, known as a master. No one volunteers to be a slave. People are forced into slavery and held in it by the greater power of the masters.

In some cultures, slaves have some rights, the opportunity for freedom, and even the possibility of becoming community leaders. In such societies, the children of slaves might be free. In other cultures, masters treat human beings as property that can be bought and sold. The children of those slaves also become slaves with no hope of escape.

THE TRANSATLANTIC SLAVE TRADE

Transatlantic means across the Atlantic Ocean. The term *transatlantic slave trade* describes the removal by force of 10 million to 15 million people from Africa over a period from about 1400 to 1900. These Africans were shipped like animals across the Atlantic Ocean to North and South America. They were forced to work without pay in European colonies there and later in some independent nations such as the United States and Brazil.

This illustration shows African slave raiders consulting with European slave traders as slaves are inspected and forced aboard a slave ship bound for the Americas.

The peak years of the transatlantic slave trade were about 1700 to 1800. In this century, an average of 50,000 Africans each year were packed into slave ships, also known as slavers, and sent to the Americas. Until 1820, more than three times as many enslaved Africans as free Europeans traveled across the Atlantic to the lands that Europeans called the "New World."

The transatlantic slave trade was a very complicated business. Over five centuries, it involved hundreds of ships and millions of people on five continents. Merchants had to gather trade goods in Europe or Asia and ship them to Africa. The goods would be exchanged with African traders for slaves. The slaves had to be transported across thousands of miles of ocean to North America, South America, or the Caribbean. The ships then returned to Europe filled with export products to be sold there. This complex slave trade had an enormous effect on the history of Africa, the United States, South America, Europe, and the Caribbean.

THE IMPORTANCE OF STUDYING THE TRANSATLANTIC SLAVE TRADE

Studying the past is one way to understand and solve the problems of the present. Like all people, today's Americans are still greatly affected by the history of events that happened long before their time.

White Europeans and Americans used racism to defend the African slave trade. They reserved slavery in the Americas only for people with dark skin. Racism remains one of the world's biggest problems. Understanding the cause of a problem is often the first step in coming up with a solution.

In addition, people scattered all over the world have ancestors whose lives were affected by the transatlantic slave trade. Many people with African ancestors now live in South

America, the Caribbean, and the United States. For example, about 95 percent of all modern-day Jamaicans are of partial African descent. Brazil has the world's largest black population outside Africa. The United States probably received less than 4 percent of all the slaves sent across the Atlantic Ocean—but this was still about 400,000 human beings. Almost all dark-skinned people in the United States in some way can trace their ancestry back to this horrible trade. Ignoring the slave trade means ignoring a major part of the heritage of millions of people.

Many people speak of the United States as a land of liberty. Yet the hundreds of thousands of Africans who lived in slavery there did not choose to immigrate to find freedom or wealth. Instead, slave traders captured them and brought them there in chains. These Africans and their descendants lived as slaves for centuries. They were forced to work so others could become wealthy. By growing sugarcane, tobacco, rice, and cotton, slaves created the enormous wealth that built the United States. They were not paid for this work, and they almost never received the credit they deserved. These African-American slaves kept alive some parts of their native African culture and created a new black culture that sustained them through centuries of hardship. In the end, the United States is a richer place for their strength and determination over the years.

1

The Earliest Forms of Slavery

Slave traders watch over their captives at a slave market in Cairo, Egypt.
Slavery existed in Africa long before the beginning of the slave trade to
the Americas.

ANCIENT SLAVES

Between 1400 and 1900, somewhere between 10 million and 15 million people were taken from Africa and shipped across the Atlantic Ocean to work in the fields and houses of the Americas. However, slavery existed long before there was even any written history to record it. In many places in the ancient world, people could become slaves by committing certain crimes, by being captured in wars or slave raids, by being sold by their parents, or by being the children of slaves. Slavery could also be a punishment when people could not repay their debts.

Slavery seems to have been common in the ancient Middle East. Around 1750 B.C., the famous law code of the Babylonian king Hammurabi ordered death for anyone helping a slave escape, as well as for anyone hiding a runaway slave. In ancient Egypt, pharaohs, or kings, used slave labor to build large buildings such as temples and perhaps some of the pyramids.

EARLY EXAMPLES OF SLAVERY

The ancient Greeks, who lived around 450 B.C., are famous as the inventors of democracy. However, slaves were an important part of the Greek world. The Greek capital city of Athens could not have existed as it did without the slaves who worked as house servants, craftspeople, shopkeepers, miners, farm workers, and sailors. In 450 B.C., slaves probably made up about one-quarter to one-third of Athens's population of 300,000.

In ancient Rome, slavery was also widely practiced. There may have been 2 million slaves in the area that is now present-day Italy at the time of Julius Caesar (40 B.C.). One hundred years later, one out of every three people in Italy was probably a slave. Most Romans assumed that slavery was an acceptable and even necessary part of society.

Slavery existed in most ancient cultures around the world. Slavery was common in the Americas before 1500. Some Central and South American people captured defeated enemies and made them slaves. This type of slavery was not based on skin color, and it was not always permanent.

In many areas of Asia, slavery was widely practiced as well. Slavery existed in China as early as 1500 B.C. During the Han Dynasty (206 B.C. to A.D. 25), slaves made up about 5 percent of the population of China. Slavery continued to be practiced in China through 1900. Slavery was also common in ancient India; there were still about 5 million slaves in India in the early 1800s.

Slavery also existed in Africa for centuries. Many Africans became slaves by being captured in wars. Some families also sold children in exchange for food in times of famine.

Some Should Rule and Others Be Ruled

Aristotle, an important ancient Greek philosopher, tried to justify the slave system. In his Politics, he divided the world into Greeks and non-Greeks (whom he called "barbarians"). He believed that it was acceptable to capture and enslave anyone who was not a Greek. Aristotle wrote that "from the hour of their birth, some are marked out for slavery, others for rule."

Occasionally, Africans were enslaved when they owed money. In West Africa, owning slaves was one of the most noticeable ways to show personal wealth. Slaves in West Africa were treated as property, but they did keep some rights, such as the right to marry. Their children were usually free.

In this picture, an African slave trader leads his captives to be sold.

Even before 1500, black slaves from Africa were widely traded throughout the Mediterranean area, the Middle East, and Asia. As many as 3 million African slaves may have been sent to the Mediterranean and the Middle East before 1500.

SLAVERY IN THE EUROPEAN MIDDLE AGES

After the fall of the Roman Empire (ca. A.D. 500), large estates in Europe broke up into small farms. In the period from 500 to 1500, known as the Middle Ages, landowners made more money from collecting rents than from farming the large plots of land themselves. In northern Europe, landowners used serfs instead of slaves. In general, serfs were poor farmers who were bound to the land because of debts they owed to the landowner for rent and supplies. European serfs had to work for the lord of the manor whenever he demanded. However, they or their children could not be bought or sold like cattle. By custom, a serf's right to the land passed to the children.

At this time, slavery also continued to be common in the region that bordered the Mediterranean Sea. These areas were mostly Islamic. The religion of Islam was founded in the early 600s. Beginning in the 630s, Muslim armies swept across India, North Africa, and Spain. Under Islamic law, prisoners captured in a jihad (holy war) could be enslaved. Muslim rulers in Africa sometimes captured slaves by claiming that their raids were jihads. They sold some of these African slaves to other Islamic areas such as Persia (present-day Iran) and Arabia. Others were sold to Christians in what are now Spain, Portugal, and Italy. As Christians slowly reconquered Spain in the 1400s, they enslaved Muslims as well.

By the time Christopher Columbus sailed for North America in 1492, slavery no longer existed in England, Holland, and most of France but remained in Spain and

Portugal. These European nations would all establish colonies in the Americas. All would adopt the slave system in their colonies and join in the African slave trade.

THE COMMERCIAL REVOLUTION

In the 1400s, changes known as the "commercial revolution" swept across Europe. Banks became much larger, and people began to use money instead of bartering, or trading, for goods. Across western Europe, kings and princes joined with bankers and merchants to encourage foreign trade and local manufacturing. Cities grew larger and nation-states such as Spain, France, and Portugal—and later, Holland and England—became much wealthier and stronger.

The Portuguese took the lead in the commercial revolution. Improvements in navigation and seafaring aided Portuguese sailors. In the 1400s, the Portuguese explored the west coast of Africa, looking for a way to the riches of Asia. In 1488, Bartholomew Diaz rounded the Cape of Good Hope at the southern tip of Africa. Ten years later, Vasco da Gama sailed all the way to India under a Portuguese flag.

As the Portuguese sailed down the coast of Africa, they began to trade with Africans for gold, nuts, fruits, olive oil, and slaves. African slaves had appeared in Europe as early as the 1300s, but the first major shipment—235 African slaves to Portugal—took place in 1444. By 1460, more than 700 African slaves were being carried to Portugal every year. The slave trade slowly became a key part of the commercial revolution.

CHRISTIAN AND ISLAMIC VIEWS OF SLAVERY

Before 1500, slavery was not based on skin color in Europe, the Middle East, Africa, Asia, or the Americas. The Greeks and Romans did not think of "race" in the same way as later Europeans did. Most slaves were prisoners of war or sold into slavery as a punishment for a crime. It made no difference to the buyers or sellers if the slaves had light or dark skin.

However, Europeans had many negative stereotypes of Africans before the era of the slave trade. Skin color was one feature that made Europeans prejudiced against Africans. In the 1400s and 1500s, many Portuguese and Spanish also believed that Africans must be inferior because they were not Christians.

The need to justify African slavery led to a huge increase in European racism. Christian Europeans claimed that they were actually helping the Africans by chaining them together and transporting them across the ocean into a lifetime of slavery under Christian masters. The kings and queens of Europe and the leaders of the Christian churches did not tell them otherwise.

Most of the European people involved in the slave trade—whether buyers, sellers,

The English word *slave* has no connection to skin color. The word first appears in the English language about 1300. It comes from the medieval Latin *sclavus,* which not only means a slave but also a Slav. The Slavs were people of eastern Europe who were conquered in the 800s and often sold as slaves.

bankers, or sailors—were Christians. The leaders of Europe who would sponsor the slave trade all were closely connected to Christian churches. Until the mid-1700s, almost all Christians accepted slavery as part of society.

In theory, Christianity would seem to be opposed to slavery. Jesus Christ once said that "whatever you wish that men would do to you, do so to them; for this is the law." But Jesus never spoke out directly against slavery. A famous passage from the Bible told slaves to "be obedient to those who are your earthly masters, with fear and trembling." The early Christian Church did not oppose Roman slavery. Instead, it preached that slaves could look forward to freedom in the next world (heaven). In the meantime, they should follow the example of Jesus, who suffered in silence, rather than using force to fight back.

Some African kings who converted to Islam cooperated in the sale of slaves. The Koran (Qur'an), the holy book of Islam, did not abolish slavery. In fact, Muhammad, the founder and prophet of Islam, owned slaves. The religious rulers who came after Muhammad discouraged the enslavement of free Muslims. However, Islam, like Christianity, found a way to make peace with the slave system. Almost all Islamic societies permitted slavery.

EUROPEANS COME TO THE AMERICAS

Slavery never became widespread in Europe, although nobles and wealthy people sometimes purchased African slaves. In general, the many poor people of Europe claimed most work for themselves. However, once Europeans invaded the Americas, they often considered slaves as possible trade goods. In 1492, Christopher Columbus, reporting to King Ferdinand and Queen Isabella of Spain about the lands he had found, wrote that he could give them "slaves, as many as they shall order." On his second voyage, Columbus loaded 500 American Indians aboard ships returning to Spain. About 200 of them died on the voyage; the other 300 were forced into slavery.

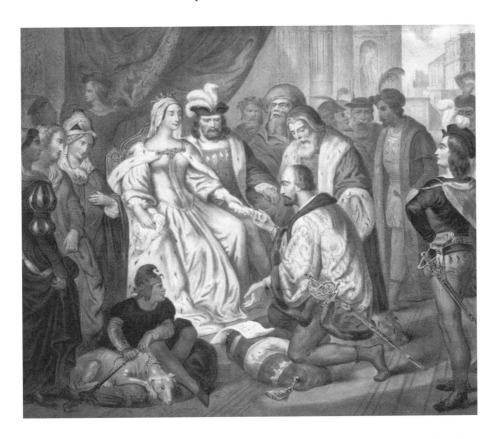

This painting shows Queen Isabella with Christopher Columbus kneeling before her. After sailing to the Americas, Columbus forced American Indians into slavery.

Bartolomé de Las Casas was a high-ranking Christian churchman in the new Spanish colonies. In 1542, he wrote to King Carlos I of Spain to complain about the brutal treatment of the Indians. According to Las Casas, "the Spanish so despised the Indians . . . that they used them not like beasts, for that would have been tolerable, but looked upon them as if they had been the dung and filth of the earth." His efforts led to laws protecting the American Indians of the Spanish colonies. Unfortunately, Las Casas's desire to protect Indians led him to support the use of Africans as slaves. In 1535, Las Casas suggested to the king that "His Majesty should send to each on the islands 500 or 600 blacks or whatever number seems appropriate." He later regretted his support for African slavery.

At first, Spanish conquerors in the early 1500s, such as Hernán Cortés in Mexico and Francisco Pizarro in Peru, simply murdered American Indians and stole everything of value. Later, the Spanish often tried to enslave the natives. In the mines of South America and the fields of the Caribbean, Europeans treated local people so harshly that some local populations were completely wiped out. A Spanish official in Mexico wrote to King Carlos I of Spain in 1544, "In the end, if Your Majesty abolishes local slavery . . . there will be no alternative to allowing blacks into the land, at least in the mines."

Europeans noticed that the New World possessed vast natural resources and land perfect for farming. The potential for wealth was enormous, if only workers could be found to labor in newly planted sugar fields and on tobacco and coffee plantations. The era of the transatlantic slave trade was about to begin.

2

Sugar and the Transatlantic Slave Trade

This illustration depicts slaves at work collecting sugarcane in a Caribbean sugar field. Beginning in the 1600s, Europeans used slaves to produce as much sugar as possible in the Americas for markets in Europe.

SUGAR PRODUCTION GROWS

After Columbus landed in the Western Hemisphere in 1492, Europeans looked to quickly make money from the newly discovered lands. The fastest way was to grow sugarcane and then export large amounts of sugar to Europe. Before 1500, Europeans had only honey and fruit juice to sweeten their food. The production of sugar in the New World was the driving force behind the slave trade.

Growing sugarcane was difficult and expensive, but a planter could make a great deal of money if he grew enough of it. Soon, plantations developed in South America and the Caribbean. A plantation was a large farm that grew a great amount of a single type of crop. Gangs of workers did the planting, hoeing, and harvesting under the supervision of an overseer. At this time, plantations in the Americas grew tobacco and coffee, but their main crop was sugarcane.

LABOR SHORTAGE ON THE SUGAR PLANTATIONS

Plantation owners needed many unskilled workers. However, few Europeans wanted to move to the Americas to work on sugar plantations. Planting and harvesting sugarcane under the hot tropical sun was hard work. The economy was improving in Europe, so people did not want to take the risk of crossing the ocean without a good chance of owning land. In 1550, it looked like European settlement of the Western Hemisphere would be very slow.

Plantation owners in South America and the Caribbean tried making slaves of American Indians, but the plan did not work well. The Indians died by the millions of European diseases against which they had no natural immunity. Also, once enslaved, they knew the land and could easily escape. On many Caribbean islands, there were not enough Indians to work plantations.

EUROPEANS TURN TO AFRICAN SLAVES

Because plantation owners could not get enough European or American Indian workers, they began to import African slave labor. African slaves cost more at first than free workers. They had to be purchased in Africa and shipped across the Atlantic Ocean. However, masters owned their slaves and could buy and sell them as if they were animals. The dark skin of Africans made it difficult for them to escape, since they could easily be identified.

In the 1600s, the Spanish, Portuguese, British, Dutch, and French began pouring Africans into their colonies in Brazil and the Caribbean. In the 1700s, English sailors began calling the voyage of slave ships from Africa to the Caribbean "the Middle Passage" because it was the middle part of a triangular route. European ships sailed to Africa with trade goods. After trading these goods to Africans for slaves, Europeans then carried the slaves across the Atlantic Ocean to the Americas. The ships then returned to Europe—sometimes empty and sometimes with sugar as cargo.

By the mid-1700s, about 1.4 million slaves worked on the production of sugar. The slave trade became a major part of the economy of four continents, employing thousands of people and involving millions of dollars. By using African slave labor on plantations, Europeans made large profits that they could never have made from small settler farms.

THE SLAVE TRADE IN AFRICA

Africa is a continent with many different kinds of land and climates—large deserts, grassy plains, and tropical rain forests. In West Africa in 1500, there were powerful empires, such as Ghana and Mali. In the area known as Guinea, further to the south, there were smaller kingdoms, such as Benin. In 1500, most Africans farmed or worked at crafts like making pottery, weaving, and metalworking. Their cultures had well-developed governments and laws.

Many different trade routes connected the African kingdoms to each other and to Islamic North Africa. When the Portuguese first appeared in West Africa in the 1400s, the native peoples thought of them as more trading partners. The Portuguese offered guns, cloth, and iron products in exchange for slaves. The slave trade caused Africans to take European money and begin to import European products. The West African economy slowly stopped growing. Instead, many people went into slave trading.

The Europeans provided the demand for slaves but Africans themselves captured the slaves, marched them to the western coast, and sold them to Europeans. Before

1800, Europeans only operated in Africa by permission of African rulers.

European traders introduced new plants and animals to Africa. Merchants brought oranges and lemons from the Mediterranean and pigs from Europe. American corn and cassava (a root crop) replaced traditional West African foods such as millet (a cereal crop) and yams. Traders also brought sweet potatoes, peanuts, papaya, and pineapples. In many areas, the higher yields of American crops led to greater African population growth.

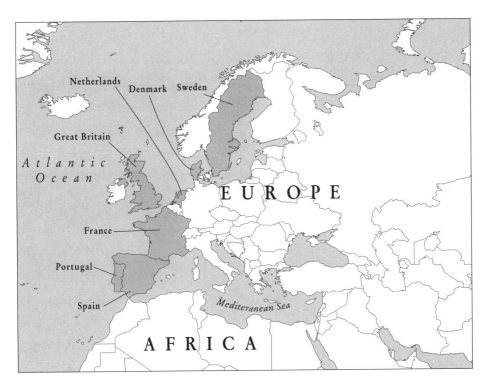

The European countries shaded on the map were those that were most involved in the slave trade to the Americas. Ships from these countries brought slaves to America and goods from the New World to their homelands.

THE SIZE OF THE AFRICAN SLAVE TRADE

Between 10 million and 15 million Africans were carried to the Americas between 1400 and 1900. Africans made up the largest group of people to come to the Western Hemisphere during that period. Less than 5 percent of all slaves were sent before 1600. Only about 14 percent arrived between 1600 and 1700. Nearly three-quarters of all African slaves (about 7 million) arrived between 1701 and 1810.

Ships from Great Britain, Portugal, and France combined to carry more than 8 million slaves to the Americas. Holland was a distant fourth, bringing about 500,000. Other slave-trading nations were Spain, Sweden, Denmark, and Germany. The American colonies—and after 1780, the United States—also participated in the slave trade.

For every slave taken captive, another may have died in the constant slave raiding in Africa or on the march to the coast. Most African slaves were young, healthy, and strong people between the ages of 15 and 30. The loss of 15 million Africans reduced the wealth and population of the continent and brought about enormous human misery.

Slave Destinations, 1451–1870

About half of all slaves went to Dutch, French, or British sugar plantations in the Caribbean. About one-third went to Portuguese Brazil, and about one-tenth to Spanish America. Only about one in 20 slaves was sent from Africa to the British colonies of North America.

SLAVERY IN BRAZIL

Portugal dominated the slave trade in the 1500s. At first, the Portuguese sent African slaves to sugar plantations on their island colonies in the eastern Atlantic, such as Madeira, Cape Verde, and the Azores. However, the Portuguese colony of Brazil eventually consumed more African slaves than any other part of the Americas.

African slaves first landed in northeast Brazil in 1538, but slaves did not arrive in large numbers to work on sugar plantations until after the 1580s. Slaves soon made up more than two-thirds of the population of northeastern Brazil. Brazil was the major market for African slaves until the early 1600s, when it was surpassed by the sugar islands in the Caribbean.

The death rate for slaves in Brazil was very high. Plantation owners could not keep up the slave population without constantly importing new slaves. Brazil therefore had a very high proportion of recently arrived slaves from Africa. Frei Antonio Vieira, a 17th-century Jesuit missionary, said that Brazil had "the body of America and the soul of Africa."

THE ENGLISH IN THE CARIBBEAN

England was slow to take advantage of the land and people of the Western Hemisphere. The English did not even have a colony in the Caribbean until they settled the islands of St. Kitts and Barbados in the 1620s. Then they planted colonies on the islands of Nevis, Montserrat, Antigua, Tobago, and St. Lucia and conquered Jamaica from the Spanish in 1655.

Most of these West Indian islands were perfect for growing sugarcane. However, plantation owners could not get enough English workers there under any conditions. British plantation owners on the islands quickly turned to slave labor.

John Newton (1725–1807)

John Newton was an English minister who wrote many hymns, including "Amazing Grace." Before that, however, he was a sailor and captain of a slave ship. Newton's mother died when he was seven years old. At age 11, he went to sea with his father. His many adventures included living for 15 months as a half-starved servant of a slave trader in Africa. He later commanded a slave ship for six years.

In 1788, John Newton wrote an autobiography of his life as a slave trader. He said that participating in the slave trade "gradually brings a numbness upon the heart, and renders most of those who are engaged in it too indifferent to the sufferings of their fellow human beings." In 1748, Newton had a religious experience and became a serious Christian. He returned to Liverpool to study Greek and Hebrew and worked to abolish slavery and the slave trade. In "Amazing Grace," he wrote, "I once was lost, but now am found; was blind but now I see."

The English entered the slave trade beginning with the African voyages of John Hawkins in the 1560s. However, the English did not become major slave carriers until the founding of the Royal African Company in 1672. The Royal African Company was located in London, England, and supported by the English government. It was the only legal slave-trading company in England until 1698. In that year,

England opened the slave trade to private merchants, many of whom had been smuggling Africans into the British colonies already. Soon, hundreds of slave ships from Liverpool and Bristol competed with ships from London.

BARBADOS AND JAMAICA

In 1638, there were 6,000 Europeans and 200 Africans living on Barbados. Then the British on Barbados began raising sugarcane. In 1660, there were 26,000 Europeans and 27,000 Africans on Barbados. In a single year between August 1664 and August 1665, Barbados exported 28 million pounds (12.7 million kg) of raw sugar. By 1680, Barbados was the wealthiest of England's American colonies. The island averaged 265 slaves per square mile (2.6 km²), compared to two slaves per square mile in recently conquered Jamaica.

However, by 1700, Jamaican plantation owners had imported more than 250,000 Africans. In 1760, there were 173,000 slaves in Jamaica, while its white population was less than 10,000. At its sugar peak, Jamaica had 700 sugar plantations worked by 105,000 slaves.

Slaves in these colonies did not have many children because men outnumbered women by a 2 to 1 margin. In addition, tens of thousands of Africans died from epidemics of yellow fever, smallpox, and measles. Thousands more died from hard work, terrible living conditions, and a poor diet. These losses did not bother the European masters. Some planters worked their slaves to death and then imported more. From 1708 to 1735, about 85,000 Africans were brought to Barbados, but the total black population only increased from 42,000 to 46,000. More than 80,000 African slaves died in Barbados in those 27 years.

The slave trade had an enormous effect on the Caribbean. About 95 percent of all modern-day Jamaicans, 90 percent of Barbadians, 90 percent of the residents of St. Kitts, and 40 percent of Trinidadians are of partial African descent.

INVESTING IN THE SLAVE TRADE

Slave trading was expensive. It was costly to supply a ship, hire a crew, and assemble the trade goods, and it took about four months to do so. A slave ship returned to Europe about 16 months after it had set out. At that point, the crew had to be paid their back wages in cash. Then the owners sold the cargo to local shipping merchants.

Most slaves were sold on credit in the Americas. If the slave ship owners wanted to make a profit, they had to wait to be paid. It could take anywhere from two to six years until they received this money. Planters did not usually pay their debts in money. Instead, they sent colonial goods that the Europeans had to sell once they arrived in Europe.

European merchants who wanted to trade in slaves often formed small trading companies of two to five people. Sometimes merchants would sell "parts of the expedition" to outside investors. These investors would lend the partners some of the money to finance the trip and receive a percentage of the profits.

The captain of a privately owned slave ship was allowed to take 5 percent of the slaves for himself. For captains, the possible profit from slave trading was much greater than their small salary. For example, Captain Pierre Mary of the *Diligent* earned 1,800 French livres (approximately $18,000 today) for a slaving voyage in 1731. In Africa, he purchased 26 slaves at about 200 livres each. He hoped to sell them in Martinique for 950 livres each. The profit from the sale of just three of the 26 slaves would be higher than Mary's salary for the entire voyage.

Slaves were often treated cruelly on the voyage to the Americas, and many died.

Cities like Liverpool in England and Nantes in France became famous as centers of slave trading. These cities had bustling ports, showy mansions, and new buildings all paid for through the trade in human beings.

A RISKY BUSINESS

The slave trade favored wealthy traders with several ships. The losses from any one slaving voyage would be covered by profits from others. Small traders who depended on a single 16-month voyage were more like gamblers than businesspeople.

The slave trade was more unpredictable than carrying other cargoes across the ocean. Ships often ran aground in unfamiliar African waters. A high death rate for slaves affected profits. Although slave ships were smaller, they carried 60 percent more crew than merchant ships. Crews on slave ships died at almost the same rate as slaves. The large crews were needed to prevent slave rebellions, which sometimes occurred anyway. This was all in addition to the usual dangers of storms, natural disasters, and pirates. In a sample of 24,259 slave-trading voyages, almost one of five ships never made it to America.

Slave trade profits seem to have averaged about 10 percent of the money invested. This was a good but not extremely high rate of profit. Investment in the slave trade was profitable, but the profit was not huge compared to sugar, textiles, coal, iron, canal-building, or shipping.

3

The Slave Trade in North America

This print, which may have been engraved around 1830, was taken from a copper plate that had been found years before. It shows a group of chained slaves being sold from one trader to another.

TOBACCO

The British colonies on the east coast of North America were different from the British colonies in the Caribbean. Unlike the West Indies, Britain's American colonies did not have the climate or the soil to raise sugarcane. However, there was far more land in North America than in the Caribbean.

After 1612, American planters in the Chesapeake colonies of Virginia, Maryland, and Delaware discovered that tobacco would grow very well there. In one way, tobacco was even better for making money than sugar was. Because tobacco was habit-forming (although this was unknown at the time), it was very hard for people to stop smoking it once they started.

Chesapeake tobacco planters, like West Indian sugar planters, needed land and workers. The planters simply stole the land from American Indians. Finding workers was more difficult. Enslaved Africans were only one possible answer to the shortage of workers in the Chesapeake. Although slavery came very early to British North America, it was not an important part of the colonial economy until 1680.

In 1616, American planters exported 2,500 pounds (1,135 kg) of tobacco to England. In the 1660s, they were exporting 20 million pounds (9 million kg). By 1771, American planters exported 105 million pounds (47.6 million kg).

THE FIRST SLAVES IN BRITISH NORTH AMERICA

John Rolfe was the first planter to grow a superior strain of tobacco in Virginia. In 1619, Rolfe reported that "a Dutch man of war [warship] that sold us twenty Negars" came to Jamestown, Virginia. Thirty years later, about 400 Africans—about 2 percent of the population—lived in the Chesapeake colonies. At the same time, there were 10,000 slaves living in the British colony of Barbados in the Caribbean.

The first Africans to be sold in North America arrived in Jamestown, Virginia, in 1619, but records are unclear as to whether they were slaves or indentured servants.

Many American planters in the 1600s thought that buying slaves was too expensive. In 1664, Maryland governor Charles Calvert wrote that he could not find a hundred planters who would promise to take one slave a year. He wrote that the planters would love to own African slaves if only they could afford them.

However, there was an American Indian slave trade in British America. The early economy of South Carolina used many American Indians as slaves. Indian groups raided weaker neighbors in search of slaves who were exchanged in Charlestown, South Carolina, for trade goods. Between 20,000 and 50,000 Indians were sold into slavery through Charlestown from 1670 to 1715.

INDENTURED SERVANTS

Instead of slaves, Chesapeake planters tried using indentured servants to work on the tobacco plantations. Indentured servants were like temporary slaves. They agreed to work for a master, usually for five to seven years, before receiving their full freedom. In many cases, the master paid the money for the ship passage that brought the indentured servant to America in the first place. However, in the early 1600s, the words *servant* and *slave* were often interchangeable.

Migration to the Chesapeake

Between 1640 and 1700, about 80,000 English indentured servants moved to Virginia, and thousands more moved to Maryland. About three out of every four English migrants to the Chesapeake during the 1600s were indentured servants. Most of them were males under 25 years of age. Half of all indentured servants died before receiving their freedom.

Because people died so quickly in the Chesapeake in the early 1600s, it did not make economic sense for a planter to buy slaves for life. It was better to hire an indentured servant for seven years, since the servant could produce as much as five times his or her purchase price in a single year. In 1670, indentured servants were still the main labor source in the Chesapeake.

AFRICANS REPLACE INDENTURED SERVANTS

After 1670, the number of people willing to come to the Chesapeake began to shrink. Conditions improved in England. Poor people saw no need to risk their lives as indentured servants in America. Many of those who did arrive went to new British colonies such as Pennsylvania and New York. Indentured servants also became free after a certain number of years. The newly freed servants did not want to stay on as hired hands. The shortage of indentured servants in the Chesapeake meant that their price began to rise.

By this time, ships from England appeared regularly in Chesapeake Bay with cargos of slaves. Britain's sugar colonies in the Caribbean, like Barbados and Jamaica, were already based on slave labor. Chesapeake planters believed that Africans were better suited than white indentured servants to hard work in a difficult climate. Colonel Landon Carter, a wealthy Virginia tobacco planter in the mid-1700s, wrote, "Those few servants that we have don't do as much as the poorest slaves we have." If profit was more important than human lives, it made perfect sense for the Chesapeake planters to switch to slave labor.

In this picture, slaves on a tobacco plantation work to free plants from worms.

White Europeans had treated the first Africans in America much like indentured servants. However, in 1662, the Virginia legislature had declared that slavery was an "inheritable status according to the condition of the mother." Now the children of all enslaved women were slaves. This supply of labor, which was possibly never-ending, gave landowners an even better reason to invest in slaves.

Enslaving Africans was not just a matter of money and profit but also of racism. Europeans believed that black-ness of skin color meant evil and the devil. White prisoners of war and criminals were sometimes used as forced labor, but they were never treated as slaves in the same way Africans were. Slavery in North America was reserved for people with dark skin.

In 1676, poor whites in the Virginia backcountry rebelled against the power of the coastal planters. This was called Bacon's Rebellion. Planters loyal to the royal governor put down Bacon's Rebellion, but it made them worry about future revolts from the poor whites. The use of African slaves, however, helped the planters bond together with the poor whites. Both groups shared a belief that light-skinned people were better than dark-skinned people. For this reason, even poor whites had a stake in the slave system.

SLAVERY IN THE CHESAPEAKE BAY AREA

In 1700, the number of enslaved blacks in the Chesapeake had risen to 10,000, or about 10 percent of the population. By 1720, there were 32,000, or about 20 percent. By 1750, there were 120,000 slaves in Virginia alone—almost 40 percent of the colony's population. Indentured servants almost completely disappeared. In 1770, three out of every five English families in the Chesapeake owned at least one slave. By then, there were half a million slaves in the American South.

English common law in 1600 did not recognize the ownership of one human being by another. This meant that American colonists had to create their own laws regarding slavery. Legislatures in the Chesapeake colonies began to pass laws taking away the rights of Africans. One observer noted that in the English colonies in America, "these two words, Negro and Slave," were almost synonyms.

Growing tobacco was not as hard work as raising sugarcane or sugar beets. Slaves were less likely to die from a disease or overwork in the Chesapeake colonies than in the West Indies. Because tobacco profits were lower than sugar profits, Chesapeake planters could not constantly buy new slaves. They looked at their slaves as a long-term investment. Some tobacco planters tried to increase their workforce by purchasing high numbers of female slaves and encouraging large families. By the middle of the 1700s, the African population in America was increasing naturally. Unlike the Caribbean islands, British North America did not depend on the slave trade to replace the supply of slaves.

SLAVERY IN GEORGIA AND SOUTH CAROLINA

Europeans imported African slaves into every North American colony. However, slaves were most common in the tobacco-growing region around Chesapeake Bay and the rice-producing areas of Georgia (founded in 1733) and the South Carolina coast. Cotton did not become an important crop until after 1800.

The low country of South Carolina had a climate similar to the climate of the Caribbean. Land-hungry whites from Barbados settled the colony. They imported many slaves from areas of West Africa where growing rice was common. By 1720, two out of every three residents of South Carolina were slaves. Of all the colonies in British North America, South Carolina was the only one with a black majority.

Indigo is a purple dye that was in demand in Great Britain in the 1700s. Slaves in South Carolina and Georgia grew indigo. Exports of indigo rose from 138,000 pounds (62,600 kg) in 1747 to 1,122,000 pounds (509,000 kg) in 1774.

Growing rice in swampy lowlands was harder for slaves than farming tobacco. Slaves in South Carolina had a high death rate from diseases such as malaria and yellow fever. However, American exports of slave-grown rice increased from 10,000 pounds (4,500 kg) in 1698 to 84 million pounds (38 million kg) in 1770. Some citizens of South Carolina in the 1700s grew rich as rice planters.

These slaves are shown working on swampy rice flats.

SLAVERY IN NORTHERN AMERICA

About 10 percent of Africans coming to British North America entered northern port towns such as New Amsterdam, which would become New York City, and

Newport, Rhode Island. In 1660, New Amsterdam was the most important slave port in North America. In the North, slaves worked as servants, craftspeople, or farmhands. In 1710, there were almost 2,000 Africans living in New England, about 2 percent of the population.

Slaves were typical in the Dutch colony of New Netherland (later the English colony of New York). At the end of Dutch rule in 1664, there were probably about 800 African slaves in New Netherland. They made up about 10 percent of the population of the colony. When the English conquered New Netherland, they accepted the Dutch slave system. By 1746, New York's 9,000 adult slaves made up the largest slave population of any English colony north of Maryland.

THE GROWTH OF THE AMERICAN SLAVE TRADE

The slave trade started slowly in British North America but picked up in the 1680s and surged from the 1730s until the American Revolution (1775–1783). In 1680, people of African descent made up less than 5 percent of the American population. This percentage rose almost every year, peaking at 21 percent in 1770. The slave trade continued after the American Revolution until the legal slave trade ended in 1807.

Less than 5 percent of the total number of slaves sent from Africa were imported into British North America (and then the United States). Yet by 1825, the United States had the largest slave population of any country in the Western Hemisphere.

4

The Middle Passage

Slave traders walk among their captives on the ship *Gloria*
as it sails the Middle Passage.

SLAVE RAIDING IN AFRICA

The business of raiding towns for slaves was left almost completely to the native Africans. Europeans could not force any kingdom in Africa to enter the slave trade if it did not want to. Some areas of Africa, such as the kingdom of Benin, did remain closed to the slave trade for two centuries. However, the increasing demand (and prices) for slaves influenced African rulers to participate. African abolitionist Ottobah Cugoano was sold into slavery in the mid-1700s. He complained, "I must own to the shame of my countrymen that I was first kidnapped and betrayed by [people of] my own complexion."

In general, Europeans stayed on the western coast of Africa. They did not go inland for fear of disease and because they were greatly outnumbered. By the early 1700s, Europeans had built more than 25 trading forts along the coast near present-day Ghana. However, in the mid-1700s, small clusters of huts on shore replaced the large forts of trading companies. In these huts, independent traders operated with the help of local African rulers. European slave traders often married African women. In many areas, a group of traders with mixed ancestry ran the slave trade.

THE MARCH TO THE COAST

Until 1600, most African slaves sold to Europeans lived within 50 miles (80 km) of the west coast. As the demand for slaves increased, the slave trade reached deeper into Africa.

Some African kingdoms assembled large armies that would burn whole towns and take hundreds of prisoners as slaves. It was more common, however, for smaller groups of armed men to make raids.

African traders often delivered slaves hundreds of miles to the coast. The slaves were tied together, sometimes in groups of 50 or more. Groups of chained slaves, known as coffles, were a common sight in Africa in the 1700s. Torn from their villages, many captives died of hunger, thirst, exhaustion, or suicide on these trips.

A coffle is marched to the African coast, while the slave traders slaughter a captive who is sick or injured.

Venture Smith, an African born in Guinea in 1729, was eight years old when he was captured. Many years later, he still remembered the attack on his village, the torture and murder of his father, and the long march to the coast. He wrote, "The shocking scene is to this day fresh in my mind and I have often been overcome thinking about it." Smith was sold for 4 gallons (15 l) of rum and a piece of cloth.

THE BARRACOON AND THE TRADING POST

On the coast, slave traders kept the captives in dark dungeons or open slave pens known as barracoons. A Dutch observer noted that "markets of men are kept here in the same manner as those of beasts with us." Slave traders, sometimes called factors, lived at each trading post. The factors represented either their country or the company that sent them there. The trading posts were often guarded by soldiers.

Slave ships could not simply sail into a port, load up with slaves, and sail away. The slave traders had to visit the local ruler, ask permission to trade in his kingdom, and offer gifts. Usually, slave traders had to wait in one place for several weeks before factors and African traders rounded up enough slaves to make trading worthwhile. It was not unusual for a ship to have to visit four different locations in order to purchase 500 slaves. Most slaves spent six months to a year from the time of their capture until they boarded European ships. They would usually spend three of these months waiting on the coast.

At the barracoon, the ship's captain or doctor examined the captives. According to a Dutch slave trader, the captives to be inspected were "naked too, both men and women, without the least distinction or modesty." The slaves might be ordered to do some exercise. They were carefully checked for disease.

The captives selected to be shipped across the ocean were branded with a hot iron on the back, buttocks, or breast with the mark of the buyer. In some cases, slaves who were rejected were killed.

Olaudah Equiano was captured in 1756. In the 1780s, he wrote one of the only books to give an African's view of what it felt like to be enslaved. At his capture, Equiano thought that he "had gotten in a world of bad spirits and that they were going to kill me. . . . I asked . . . if we were not to be eaten by those white men with horrible looks, red faces, and loose hair." A French slave trader wrote that many Africans were convinced "that we transport them into our country in order to kill and eat them."

Olaudah Equiano (ca. 1745–1797)

Olaudah Equiano was born in a village east of the Niger River in present-day Nigeria. When he was 11, slave traders captured him and took him to America. Equiano was sold to a planter in the West Indies. He then worked on many different ships sailing between the Caribbean and England. He saved enough money to buy his freedom at age 21. Equiano later traveled widely as a sailor; his journeys included a trip to the Arctic. He eventually became a Christian and worked to end slavery. In 1789, he wrote his popular life story, called *The Interesting Narrative of the Life of Olaudah Equiano.* His book became very famous.

TRADING FOR SLAVES

The cargo of trade goods sent to Africa from Europe made up more than half the cost of a slave-trading expedition. Products imported into Africa included textiles, metals, cowry shells, guns and gunpowder, alcoholic drinks, and luxury goods.

The slave trade was quite complicated. The two main goods traded by European slavers on the African coast actually came from India. Indian cloth was greatly in demand in Africa. Slave ships also brought thousands of pounds of cowry shells packed in barrels. Many West Africans used the cowry shells as money. The shells originally came from the Maldives Islands near India. Both the cotton and the cowries were shipped from India to Europe and then to Africa.

The *Diligent*'s Trade Goods

In 1731, the *Diligent* set sail from Europe to trade for slaves in Africa. Almost half of the trade goods carried by the *Diligent* consisted of cowries and Indian cloth. Another 25 percent was brandy, while guns and ammunition made up 14 percent. The rest of the trade goods were long smoking pipes from Holland and bars of Swedish iron.

The slave trade in Africa was mostly done by barter. The price of a slave would be set in terms of ounces of gold, even though the payment was made in trade goods. Buyers and sellers argued over the value of the slave and the value of the merchandise. Prices of slaves varied a great deal. However,

African traders were experts at getting the most money they could from Europeans.

After purchasing the slaves, traders would also buy supplies for the trip across the Atlantic Ocean. Common items bought from the native peoples and the trading posts included corn, kidney beans, yams, fruit, coconuts, and plantains. Fresh water for the long ocean voyage was especially important.

EUROPEAN WEAPONS IN AFRICA

The slave trade threw the African continent into chaos. Europeans encouraged Africans to fight each other and gave them powerful weapons. Neighboring African kingdoms, fearing invasion, purchased as many guns as possible. By 1730, Europeans exported about 180,000 guns a year just to western Africa. An English observer wrote that "whenever the King of Barsally wants Goods or Brandy . . . the King goes and ransacks some of his enemies' towns, seizing the people and selling them." A Dutch report from the same time explained why slaves had replaced other exports:

> The great quantity of guns and powder that the Europeans have brought here from time to time has caused terrible wars among the kings, princes, and caboceers [headmen of west African villages] of those lands, who made slaves of their prisoners of war. These slaves were increasingly bought up by Europeans at steadily increasing prices. Consequently, there is now very little trade among the coast Negroes except in slaves.

LOADING THE SLAVE SHIPS

Africans usually controlled the slaves until their sale to the ship's captain. Then the ship's crew rowed groups of slaves from the barracoons and the dungeons of coastal forts out to a waiting ship. Ottobah Cugoano wrote that "there was nothing to be heard but the rattling of chains, smacking of whips, and the groans and cries of our fellow-men. Some would not stir from the ground, when they were lashed and beat in the most horrible manner."

Thomas Phillips of the slave ship *Hannibal* recorded that many West Africans were so reluctant "to leave their own country, that they have often leaped out of the canoes, boats and ships, into the sea and kept underwater till they were drowned to avoid being taken up by our boats. . . . We had about 12 negroes did willfully drown themselves, and others starved themselves to death."

Sailors placed slaves below deck in spaces only 6 feet (1.8 m) wide and 2.5 feet (0.8 m) high. The women were usually separated from the men. Slaves were chained to each other hand and foot. Some slave ships gave the slaves more room. Their captains argued that slaves were a valuable cargo. If fewer slaves died, more profit could be made. "Tight packers" reversed this argument. They claimed that slaves were so valuable that a slave ship should carry as many as possible, no matter how many died.

In 1788, Parliament, Britain's lawmaking body, attempted to regulate slave ships so that fewer slaves would die on the Middle Passage. Parliament measured 18 Liverpool slave ships, including the *Brookes.* Thomas Clarkson, a famous British opponent of slavery, drew a picture of what the *Brookes* looked like when fully loaded with slaves. Clarkson's shocking drawing of the inhuman conditions that slaves suffered became one of the most famous pieces of evidence against the slave trade.

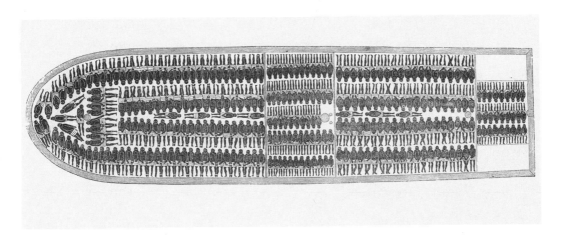

British abolitionist Thomas Clarkson drew this representation of the ship *Brookes* fully loaded with slave bodies. The illustration demonstrated the horrible living conditions for slaves on slave ships.

CROSSING THE OCEAN

The route of a slave ship depended on which region of the African coast it sailed from. A voyage from Senegambia to Barbados might take only three weeks, but some ships from Guinea or Angola that ran into storms took as long as three months to cross the Atlantic. Because of improvements in technology and organization, the length of the average voyage decreased greatly between 1600 and 1800.

Many slave ships had a daily routine. In the morning, the crew might bring the slaves on deck. They attached the men's leg irons to a great chain running the length of the ship. Women were usually left unchained. Breakfast might be beans or corn mush. Dinner would be another cheap, bland meal. Then the slaves would be led back down below. Slaves received about 2 quarts (1.9 l) of water a day. Any slaves who refused to eat might be tortured until they gave in.

Sometimes, the crew would command the slaves to jump up and down or dance on deck. This practice was called "dancing the slave." It was supposed to give the slaves some exercise. Alexander Falconbridge, a doctor on a slave ship, wrote that if slaves moved too slowly, "they are flogged [whipped], a person standing by them all the time with a cat-o'-nine tails in his hand for that purpose."

Below deck was a brutal place for slaves, even in ships with the most room. There were only about six air holes on a slaver, each one only about 5 inches (13 cm) long. When the seas became rough or there was heavy rain, even those had to be shut. Then there would be no fresh air at all below deck and the area

Below Deck

Alexander Falconbridge served as a doctor on a slave ship in the peak years of the trade. Falconbridge described the conditions that the slaves experienced below deck:

The excessive heat was . . . intolerable. The deck, that is, the floor of their rooms, was so covered with blood and mucus . . . that it resembled a slaughterhouse. It is not in the power of the human imagination to picture to itself a situation more dreadful or disgusting.

would become unbelievably hot. At night, slaves, chained together, had to sleep side by side, or "spoon" fashion. The rolling of the ship often tossed slaves around so the skin on their elbows was worn to the bone from scraping on the bare planks where they lay. Equiano wrote, "The shrieks of the women and the groans of the dying rendered the whole a scene of horror almost inconceivable."

DEATH ON THE CROSSING

Slave ships were famous for being filthy. Atlantic sailors said they could "smell a slaver five miles [8 km] down wind." There were no bathrooms below deck. The slaves were given only a few small buckets. Chained slaves who were far from the buckets often could not get to them in time. They would have to relieve themselves where they lay. In tight quarters, this led to quarrels and fighting. Some captains ordered crews to scrape and mop the holds daily, but the task was so unpleasant that it was not done on many ships. Equiano remembered that when he was first taken below deck, "I received such a salutation in my nostrils as I had never experienced in my life . . . and became so sick and low that I was not able to eat."

Many slaves started out sick while waiting for the ships to load. The main killers were smallpox, scurvy, yellow fever, malaria, and especially a type of dysentery known as the "bloody flux." There were ships' doctors, usually called surgeons, on most slavers. These doctors tried to take care of the "merchandise" but were usually of little help. Africans who died on the trip were simply thrown overboard. Sharks sometimes followed slave ships all the way across the Atlantic Ocean.

ESTIMATES OF THE MORTALITY RATE

In the five centuries of the slave trade, there were about 40,000 slaving voyages. With so many voyages, it is not surprising that slaves on different ships had very different mortality rates. The mortality rate was influenced by the location from which the ship left, the length of the voyage, and the number of women and children aboard. The most important influence was probably the condition of the slaves when they boarded.

The crews of slave ships generally tried to feed and treat the slaves decently according to the standards of the time. This was not because they cared about the slaves as people but because only a living (and healthy-looking) slave would fetch a good profit when the ship landed. However, slaves died on the Middle Passage at a much higher rate than did criminals, soldiers, and free immigrants who took similar ocean voyages.

More than 1 million slaves, about 12 percent (one out of every eight), died on the Middle Passage. In general, the mortality rate declined over time. It was about 20 percent in the early 1600s, but probably less than 10 percent by the 1800s. However, this was still an extremely high death rate for a mostly young adult population.

Besides the million slaves who died on the Middle Passage itself, even more slaves probably died in the slave raids in Africa, during the march to the coast, and while waiting in barracoons for slave ships. It is impossible to estimate these numbers with any accuracy. Nor is it possible to estimate how many slaves died immediately after being unloaded in the Americas.

A Song of the Slave Trade

Slaves sometimes sang as they marched to the coast. In this song, slaves from the African kingdom of Bornu beg one of their gods for help. This translation was still sung by slaves in the United States in the 1800s.

Bornu-land was rich and good,
Wells of water, fields of food,
Bornu land we see no longer,
Here we thirst and here we hunger,

Here the Moor man smites in anger.
Where are we going, Rubee?
Where are we going?
Where are we going?
Hear us, save us, Rubee!
Moons of marches from our eyes,
Bornu-land behind us lies.
Hot the desert wind is blowing,
Wild the waves of sand
are flowing!
Hear us! Tell us, where are we going?
Where are we going, Rubee?

SLAVE REBELLIONS

The best time for slaves to fight for their freedom was while they were still in Africa. Some of the bloodiest slave rebellions took place before the slaves were loaded onto ships. There was also some chance of escape while the ship was still in African waters. If slaves could see the coast, they could possibly reach shore.

Once at sea, however, a slave rebellion could be a disaster for everyone. If the crew members were killed, inexperienced slaves would have to try to sail the ship back to Africa or continue across the Atlantic. Still, almost one-third of shipboard rebellions took place on the high seas.

Slave ship captains and crews always worried about slave rebellions. Each ship held far more slaves than Europeans, and everyone on the ship knew it. Ship captains used a combination of punishments and rewards to keep the captives under control. The captains put down rebellions without mercy and sometimes tortured slaves after a failed rebellion. They also occasionally gave gifts of tobacco or brandy for good behavior. The best way for slave ships to avoid revolts was to get across the Atlantic as fast as possible.

Sometimes, the only possible way that slaves could resist their captors was to jump overboard and drown. These suicides alarmed the Europeans. They put large nets on the sides of ships to catch slaves who jumped overboard. Even so, Equiano saw two Africans chained together who, "preferring death to such a life of misery, somehow made through the nettings and jumped into the sea."

5

The American Slave Trade

This woodcut shows the deck of the ship *Wildfire*
crowded with slaves.

SELLING SLAVES

As a slave ship approached its destination in the Western Hemisphere, the crew prepared the Africans for the slave market. Most were freed from their chains and allowed to wash themselves. The crew shaved the heads and beards of the male captives and rubbed the slaves' skin with palm oil. The crew did everything possible to increase the Africans' selling price when they reached shore. However, the stress of the Middle Passage could not be hidden so easily. One witness described the slaves leaving the ship as "walking skeletons covered over with a piece of tanned leather."

Slaves were sold in different ways. Most slave sales in North America took place aboard the ships, although the ships' captains sometimes moved the slaves to a special warehouse on shore to make it easier for the buyers. Occasionally, one wealthy planter would buy an entire cargo of slaves. Sometimes, a merchant bought the slaves and then resold them to local buyers. Most often, slaves were sold individually to the highest bidder in a public auction. The sales took several days. Purchased slaves left with their new owners. Smart buyers reserved the right to cancel a sale if a slave proved unsatisfactory. That way, the buyer lost nothing if the slave died or ran away during the trial period.

> Slaves who were less desirable because of sickness, injury, or age were called "refuse slaves." If no one bought them, they were returned to chains. They might wait weeks until someone bought them, and many did not survive the first year in their new land.

THE SHIFT TO PRIVATE MERCHANTS

Before 1700, European governments supported national companies to control the slave trade. Great Britain organized the Royal African Company, France created the Senegal Company, and Holland had the Dutch West India Company. Each national government wanted its company to be the only one from that country allowed to trade in slaves in Africa.

African slave traders knew it was not in their best interest to deal with only one company. They played off one European nation against another to raise the price of slaves. By the 1700s, the demand for slaves in the Western Hemisphere was so high that the national companies could no longer supply it. Slowly, each European nation opened the trade up to private merchants: the British in 1698, the French in 1725, and the Dutch in 1730. By the mid-1700s, hundreds of ships off the coast of Africa competed against each other for slaves.

AMERICAN CARRIERS

The American merchants who sent out ships to carry slaves usually lived in northern port cities. The first American slave ships probably sailed from Boston in the 1630s. After 1750, Rhode Island became the center of the American slave trade. Many other New England towns, including New London, Connecticut, and Portsmouth, New Hampshire, also had a hand in buying and selling human beings.

By the mid-1700s, independent American traders had become part of the slave trade. However, American-owned vessels never played a major role in bringing African slaves to North America. British ships from London, Bristol, and Liverpool carried most slaves to the American South.

TRIANGLES

The slave trade is often remembered as a series of triangles. One triangle involved Europe, Africa, and the Caribbean. For example, from 1677 to 1678, the British ship *Arthur* traveled to Africa to buy slaves. The British paid for them with European cloth, pieces of brass, and cowry shells. The slaves were shipped to the Caribbean and sold for sugar, which was sent in the same vessel back to England.

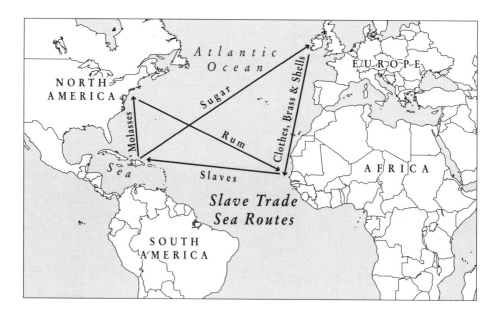

The slave trade can be imagined as a series of triangles, as shown here, but the traders and ships themselves often made single out-and-back voyages, sometimes returning empty.

Another triangle was between the Caribbean, America, and Africa. Americans would import molasses (made from sugar produced by slaves) from the West Indies. They would then turn the molasses into rum. The American colonists drank most of this rum, but merchants shipped some of it to Africa. In Africa, they would use the rum to purchase slaves to bring back to the Caribbean sugar islands. However, trade with Africa was never a large part of the American colonial economy. Most colonial American ships carried American tobacco, rice, and indigo to Great Britain and grain, fish, and lumber to the West Indies.

The idea of a "triangular" slave trade can be misleading. The slave trade was actually more like an "H" made up of single out-and-back voyages. Many European slave ships returned empty to Europe because West Indian planters preferred to ship sugar on large vessels specially designed for that purpose. These larger ships sailed back and forth to Europe but did not travel to Africa.

Seasoned Slaves

"Seasoned" slaves were slaves who lived in the Caribbean for a few months to a year. During this time, weak slaves would die, and the others would adjust to the climate of the New World. In general, American colonists did not want slaves seasoned in the West Indies. American slave owners feared that the West Indian planters were not really providing seasoned slaves but instead getting rid of difficult or unusable slaves. Colonial buyers preferred to buy slaves directly from Africa. Almost as many American slaves came directly from Africa as from the West Indies.

THE SLAVE TRADE IN MASSACHUSETTS

Many people in colonial Massachusetts depended on the slave trade, which gave work to sail makers, rope makers, tanners (leather workers), and coopers (barrel makers). Many lawyers, insurers, clerks, and scriveners (secretaries) handled the paperwork for slave merchants. Slave brokers and retail merchants brought together buyers and sellers of slaves. Colonial newspapers received money from advertisements for slaves. All over New England, loggers, livestock farmers, and fishermen provided the goods that were shipped to the West Indies and traded for slaves.

Because American revolutionaries made speeches at Faneuil Hall, John Adams later called the hall the "cradle of liberty," but it was actually built with money from the slave trade.

Many New England fortunes began with the buying and selling of slaves. Cornelius Waldo, the great-grandfather of writer Ralph Waldo Emerson, was a merchant who imported "Choice Irish Duck, fine Florence wine, negro slaves and Irish butter." Peter Faneuil inherited a fortune built on his uncle's slave trade. Faneuil gave some of this money to Boston to build Faneuil Hall. The hall was later the site of speeches by Samuel Adams and other revolutionaries that led the way to American independence. Faneuil Hall, called the "cradle of liberty" by John Adams, was constructed with money that came from the slave trade.

RHODE ISLAND SLAVE PORTS

The small colony of Rhode Island had very little farmland. Rhode Island residents relied on trade instead. In 1732, Rhode Island removed a tax on importing slaves. This resulted in a boom for slave traders. The cities of Providence, Bristol, and Newport produced many slave merchants, including the Brown family of Providence, who later would found Brown University.

In the late 1700s, Rhode Island merchants dominated the American slave trade. By 1808, Rhode Islanders had transported more than 100,000 Africans. Rhode Island towns could not compete with Europe when it came to textiles, metal wares, or guns. However, they had one product of superior quality—the rum they distilled. The Caribbean sugar islands supplied the molasses needed to make rum. In 1769, the city of Newport alone had 22 rum distilleries.

In 1774, Newport was the main northern slave market and the most important city in southern New England. At that time, Newport merchants operated more than 500 ships, including at least 50 slavers. So many Carolina planters came to Newport on vacation in the summer that the city was called the "Carolina hospital." Merchants from the city of Bristol were also involved in the slave trade.

A Slave-Trading Family

In 1744, Mark Anthony DeWolf married Abigail Potter, the sister of a slave merchant in Bristol. DeWolf and his wife had 15 children, four of whom became captains of slave ships. Seven members of this family were responsible for more than half of all slave voyages from Bristol between 1784 and 1808.

Mark Anthony's son James commanded his first slave ship at 19. He continued in the slave trade long after it became illegal in 1808. James DeWolf also experimented with whaling and trade with China. In 1821, the Rhode Island Assembly, undisturbed by his illegal slave-trading past, chose James DeWolf to be a U.S. senator. He served until 1825. In 1837, after an exciting life as both a lawbreaker and lawmaker, he died on his 1,000-acre (400-ha) Bristol estate.

JEWS AND THE SLAVE TRADE

In recent years, some historians have argued that Jews either dominated the slave trade or were highly involved as slave traders. Some Jews did participate in the Atlantic slave trade, but less than a dozen were serious traders. This group transported a very small percentage of the total number of

Africans brought to America. Most Jewish merchants preferred to import fabrics, diamonds, and silver rather than slaves.

A few merchants in colonial Rhode Island made up the largest group of Jewish slave traders in the British Empire. Aaron Lopez and his father-in-law, Jacob Rivera, were both wealthy Jewish Rhode Island merchants involved in the slave trade. Lopez was born in Portugal and arrived with his family in Newport about 1750. Within 20 years, Lopez owned or invested in more than 80 sailing vessels. Lopez was also one of the founders of the Touro Synagogue in Newport, the oldest synagogue in America. However, the Jewish merchants of Rhode Island controlled less than 10 percent of the voyages and slaves delivered by Rhode Island traders in the 1700s.

In those years, Jews supplied less than 2 percent of the money invested in the slave trade. When the British slave trade became the largest in the world, Jews represented less than 1 percent of ship owners and traders in the African slave trade. Most Jews in England's Caribbean and North American colonies lived in towns rather than on farms or plantations. They usually owned slaves at about the same rate as their non-Jewish town-dwelling neighbors.

SLAVERY IN NEW YORK

Some of New York's leading citizens, such as John Beekman, John Van Cortlandt, and Philip Livingston imported slaves. Slave auctions were held weekly and sometimes daily at several locations around New York City. From 1701 to 1726, New York officially imported more than 1,500 slaves from the

Caribbean and another 800 from Africa. The actual numbers were probably higher because people often smuggled slaves into New York along the coast of Long Island to avoid paying the tax on slaves. Most slave ships docked at New York City, but an occasional slave ship stopped at Perth Amboy, New Jersey.

New York had the largest colonial slave population north of Maryland. Between 1732 and 1754, slaves represented more than one-third of the total immigration through New York City. In 1756, slaves made up about one-quarter of the populations of New York City and Westchester County.

SOUTHERN SLAVE PORTS

South Carolina and Virginia were the main markets for slaves in America. South Carolina received about 70,000 slaves between 1735 and 1775. Virginia received about the same number between 1699 and 1775. Charleston and Richmond were both major international slave ports. Probably about two-thirds of African captives transported to America landed at ports in Virginia and South Carolina.

Many of the so-called First Families of Virginia engaged in slave trading. Benjamin Harrison, the ancestor of two American presidents, regularly imported West Indian slaves. Henry Middleton, delegate to the First Continental Congress, and Henry Laurens, president of the Second Continental Congress, were both well-known Charleston slave merchants. Nine of the first 15 American presidents were southern slave owners.

6

The United States Abolishes the Slave Trade

This woodcut from around 1840 shows an abolitionist freeing a
slave from chains. The picture appeared in an American almanac
against slavery.

THE FADING SLAVE TRADE

The transatlantic slave trade to North America peaked in the 1780s. In that decade, slave traders sent an astonishing average of 80,000 Africans every year to be slaves in the United States. Yet within 30 years, Great Britain, the United States, France, and Holland would all prohibit the African slave trade.

There are many reasons why these countries abolished the transatlantic slave trade. In the late 1700s, some people began to view slavery as evil. Europeans began to argue that slavery violated the idea of the equality of all people. Some religious groups declared that slavery contradicted Christian beliefs. A peaceful mass movement against slavery, led by William Wilberforce and Thomas Clarkson, began in Britain. Opponents of slavery picked out the Atlantic slave trade as the worst part of the slave system and, therefore, the easiest to attack.

THE INDUSTRIAL REVOLUTION

Beginning about 1750, new inventions in England made it possible to make cloth by machine. The period that followed is known as the Industrial Revolution. Before the Industrial Revolution, most people made goods in their own homes with simple tools. Afterward, most goods were made in large factories with complicated machinery. Cities grew rapidly, and Great Britain became the leading industrial country in the world.

An 18th-century print shows a silk mill during the Industrial Revolution. At this time, investors began putting money into factories instead of slaves—one factor in the decline of the transatlantic slave trade.

The slave trade did not cause the Industrial Revolution, but the slave colonies gave the British economy a major push. By the late 1700s, the British were buying many luxuries that they could not have gotten in 1650—rich fabrics, foreign foods, tobacco, tea, coffee, sugar, books, and toys. Many owners of Caribbean plantations did not live on their plantations. Instead, they hired overseers to run their plantations while they lived in Europe and spent their money on elegant city houses or large landed country estates. This rise in consumer demand led to the desire to grow even more sugar and tobacco.

Thousands of British workers labored to build ports and warehouses, refine sugar and tobacco, distill rum from molasses, and manufacture the cloth and iron products needed by people in Africa and the Americas. Shipyards built hundreds of slavers and merchant ships. In addition, British trade with Asia increased because of the need for Indian textiles and cowries to purchase slaves. All these activities set the stage for the Industrial Revolution, which then spread to the United States in the late 1700s.

However, the Industrial Revolution also led to the decline of the slave trade. Wealthy people began to invest their money in factories. The slave trade no longer seemed like such a good investment. Some Europeans and Americans believed that free labor was the best way to organize society. It was true that a slave owner did not have to pay slaves any salary but they would work only as hard as their masters forced them to work. There was no reason for them to work any harder. Slaves also could not buy goods and services to help the economy. By 1800, many people thought that slavery was outdated as an economic system.

THE QUAKERS CHANGE THEIR MINDS

The Quakers, also known as the Society of Friends, were a religious group that began in England in the mid-1600s. They believed that people should follow an "inner light" put in their own heart by God. The Quakers refused to carry weapons or fight in wars. By the mid-1700s, there were 90,000 English-speaking Quakers.

In the early 1700s, wealthy Quaker slave owners lived in the West Indies and Quaker merchants traded slaves in London, England; Newport, Rhode Island; and Philadelphia, Pennsylvania. However, other Quakers in England and America began to speak out against slavery.

In 1758, the Philadelphia Meeting of Quakers voted to pressure Quaker slave owners to stop participating in the slave trade. In 1772, Quaker Anthony Benezet wrote a famous antislavery pamphlet called *Some Historical Account of Guinea*. Benezet and another Quaker, John Woolman, made opposition to slavery a major part of Quaker thinking.

John Woolman (1720–1772)

Quaker leader John Woolman was one of the first white Americans to protest against the horrors of slavery. Woolman was born in New Jersey in 1720. He was originally a shopkeeper and a tailor. In 1754, Woolman wrote *Some Considerations on the Keeping of Negroes,* one of the earliest antislavery publications in America. He visited Quakers in many colonies to encourage them to free their slaves. Woolman wrote, "Deep-rooted customs [such as slavery], though wrong, are not easily altered; but it is the duty of all to be firm in that which they certainly know is right for them."

John Woolman was a Quaker leader who spoke out against slavery—one of the first white Americans to do so.

The Quakers were the first organized American abolitionists (people who wanted to abolish slavery). In 1790, the American Quakers petitioned the U.S. Congress for an end to slavery.

SLAVERY AND THE NEW AMERICAN NATION

In the 1760s and 1770s, the British colonies in America quarreled with their government in London. Many Americans complained that the king and Parliament were denying the colonists their rights as British citizens. They also thought that the colonies' taxes were too high. Some Americans, called Patriots, talked about making America an independent nation.

Patriots often referred to themselves as "slaves" of the British. This brought howls of laughter from England. Samuel Johnson, a famous English writer, joked, "How is it that we hear the loudest *yelps* for liberty amongst the drivers of Negroes?" From 1760 to 1775, 220,000 people arrived in British North America, and 85,000 of them were slaves. More than one out of every three newcomers to America in this period arrived in chains.

However, part of the Patriot strategy against Great Britain was to refuse to import any British products, including slaves. The colonies' First Continental Congress agreed that Americans would not import any slaves from the British after December 1, 1774, "after which time, we will wholly discontinue the slave trade."

THE SLAVE TRADE AND THE DECLARATION OF INDEPENDENCE

American colonies had often taxed imported slaves. For some colonial governments, this was a way of raising money. Others saw the tax as a way of limiting slavery. Some colonists feared slave revolts. Other Americans did not want too many dark-skinned people in America. Some people simply believed that slavery was evil.

Because the British made money from the slave trade, they disliked the colonial attempts to limit it. The British constantly pushed America to accept more slaves. Thomas Jefferson noted this in his first draft of the Declaration of Independence. One of his complaints about King George III of England was that he had sponsored the slave trade and so had violated "the most sacred rights of life and liberty" of Africans.

However, Jefferson removed this attack from the final version of the Declaration of Independence. Jefferson later explained that South Carolina and Georgia wanted to continue to import slaves, and he did not want to anger those colonies. He also claimed that he did not want to condemn the northern merchants who had been the carriers of slaves.

The Declaration of Independence stated that every person had natural rights, including liberty, but it did not criticize slavery or the slave trade. When Thomas Jefferson wrote that "all men are created equal," he owned 175 slaves. He lived off their work and did not pay them. He sold slaves to pay his debts, gave them away as gifts, and sometimes sold slaves away from their families as punishment.

Some Patriots did oppose slavery. William Livingston, Patriot governor of New Jersey, wrote that slavery was "utterly inconsistent with the principles of Christianity and humanity and in America . . . particularly . . . disgraceful."

SLAVERY AND THE U.S. CONSTITUTION

After the American Revolution, 85 percent of all mainland slaves lived in four states: Virginia (221,000), South Carolina (97,000), North Carolina (91,000), and Maryland (81,000). New York had the fifth-largest number of slaves, about 60,000 fewer slaves than Maryland.

In the summer of 1787, delegates from 12 states met in Philadelphia to write a new constitution. They tried to create a national government stronger than the first American government, but not so strong that it would turn into a dictatorship.

The new U.S. Constitution supported slavery. The famous "Three-Fifths Compromise" counted each slave as three-fifths of a person when counting the population of a state. This gave more political power to the slave states in the South. In addition, Article IV of the Constitution required each state to help return runaway slaves to their owners.

Jacob Green was a brave Presbyterian minister in New Jersey. In 1778, he delivered a sermon stating, "Can it be believed that a people contending for liberty should at the same time be supporting slavery? . . . I cannot but think that our practicing Negro Slavery is the most crying sin in our land." As a result, a New Jersey mob destroyed his church.

The slave trade, as opposed to slavery itself, had less support at the Constitutional Convention. Between 1776 and 1786, all the states except Georgia and South Carolina had either banned or heavily taxed the international slave trade. The Constitutional Convention had to decide whether the national government or each individual state government should control the slave trade.

> In 1780, four states contained 85 percent of all mainland slaves: Virginia, with 221,000; South Carolina, with 97,000; North Carolina, with 91,000; and Maryland, with 81,000. New York contained the fifth-largest number of slaves but was far behind, with 21,000.

At the convention, Rufus King of Massachusetts and Gouverneur Morris of Pennsylvania spoke out against the slave trade. Morris complained that Georgians and Carolinians went to Africa and "in defiance of the most sacred laws of humanity" they "tear away . . . fellow creatures from their dearest connections and damn them to the most cruel bondage." South Carolina's delegate, Charles Pinckney, responded, "South Carolina and Georgia cannot do without slaves. . . . An attempt to take away the right [to import slaves] will produce serious objections to the Constitution."

THE SLAVE TRADE COMPROMISE

As they did with many issues at the Constitutional Convention, the delegates solved the question of the slave trade by compromise. Roger Sherman of Connecticut said, "It was better to let the Southern states import slaves than to part with [the Southern states]." South Carolina delegate Charles Pinckney suggested that there should be no prohibition on the slave trade until 1808. At that time, the states could debate the question again.

Future U.S. president James Madison voted against the slave trade compromise at the Constitutional Convention.

James Madison, a slave-owning planter and delegate from Virginia, commented, "So long a term [twenty years] will be more dishonorable to the National character than to say nothing about it in the Constitution." However, Pinckney's suggestion passed by a vote of 7 to 4, with Pennsylvania, New Jersey, Delaware, and Virginia voting against the compromise. Georgia and South Carolina had won the day. The new U.S. Constitution prohibited the U.S. Congress from passing any law to outlaw the slave trade for 20 years.

THE LAST SLAVE BOOM

In those 20 years between 1788 and 1808, slave traders sent more than 200,000 human beings from Africa to work as slaves in the United States. That figure equaled the number of

Africans who had been brought to British North America during the entire colonial period. In just the years 1805 and 1806, Rhode Island slavers alone imported an average of 6,400 Africans a year. For a while, the United States was the third-largest slave-carrying nation in the Atlantic world, and Charleston boomed as one of the world's largest slaving ports.

Despite the supposed ideals of the American Revolution, the period from 1780 to 1810 was the height of the slave trade to North America. The slave population of the United States was three times greater in 1820 than it had been in 1775.

THE END OF IMPORTING SLAVES

In Europe, and especially in Great Britain, public opinion had turned against the transatlantic African slave trade. In 1807, Parliament made it illegal for British ships to carry slaves and for British colonies to import them. Parliament passed this law even though British slavers had carried more than 200,000 Africans between 1801 and 1807.

In the United States, there was also a strong movement to

George Mason Argues against the Slave Trade

Virginia delegate George Mason argued that the Constitution should make the slave trade illegal. He complained:

Maryland and Virginia had already prohibited the importation of slaves expressly. North Carolina had done the same in substance. All of this would be in vain if South Carolina and Georgia be at liberty to import. The Western people . . . will fill that country with slaves if they can be got through South Carolina and Georgia.

end the international slave trade (but not slavery). After fierce debate, the U.S. Congress passed a law that made it illegal to import slaves into the United States after January 1, 1808. President Thomas Jefferson signed the law on March 2, 1807.

After 1808, slaves continued to be smuggled from Africa to the United States. However, the growth of the American slave labor force in the 1800s depended mostly on slaves born in the United States. The ban on the international slave trade greatly increased the importance of the slave trade *within* the United States.

7

Internal and Illegal Slave Trading

In the late 1700s and early 1800s, cotton production in South Carolina and Georgia boomed. Plantation owners required even more slaves to work the cotton fields.

A DYING SYSTEM?

In 1790, slavery did not seem to have a bright future in the Chesapeake. After years of farming, many tobacco plantations had completely used up the nutrients in the soil. Virginia, Maryland, and Delaware planters began to switch to products that required less labor than tobacco. Slaves were no longer in demand in the Chesapeake.

Some planters began to manumit, or free, their slaves. By 1860, more than half of the African Americans in Maryland and nine-tenths of those in Delaware were free. Even in Virginia, a movement grew to manumit slaves. Between 1776 and 1808, all the northern states had abolished slavery or passed laws for gradual emancipation, or freedom. Slavery seemed to be dying out by itself. Unfortunately, American attitudes about slavery changed with the growth of the cotton industry after 1793.

THE GROWTH OF THE COTTON INDUSTRY

For hundreds of years, most Europeans wore clothes made from wool or flax. (Flax fibers were used to make linen cloth.) Cotton spinning and weaving was a very small industry. In the late 1700s, however, the new machines of the Industrial Revolution made it easy to produce cotton textiles cheaply and in large amounts. Soon, there was a tremendous demand for cotton to feed the new machines. This demand completely changed the world's economy.

In 1790, the entire United States produced only 3,000 bales of cotton. Cotton grew well in many areas of the South. However, the seeds were so difficult to remove from the fiber that it took an entire day to hand-clean a single pound (0.45 kg) of cotton.

In the 1790s, a number of inventors, including Eli Whitney, developed machines to separate the cottonseeds from the fiber. The first cotton gin was simply a hand-cranked cylinder with metal teeth, but the device allowed a worker to clean 50 pounds (23 kg) of cotton a day.

This illustration depicts slaves using an automated cotton gin. In the early 1800s, the cotton gin revolutionized the cotton industry and fueled a growing slave trade within the United States.

SLAVERY AND COTTON

The southern plantation and slave system was easily adapted to growing cotton. Planters with a lot of land and many slaves made enormous profits. Growing cotton on plantations that used slave labor changed the South. Most planters invested all their money into cotton, so there were not many factories or industries. Very few immigrants would settle in the South, since they could not work as cheaply as slaves, who were paid nothing for their labor. Only a small number of large cities developed in the South and there were not many railroads and canals. Unlike the North, the South was now a farming and slave society.

Between 1800 and 1860, about one-third of all southern white families owned slaves. Many others hoped to own them. Slave owners with many slaves were rare; the average slaveholder owned five slaves. In 1860, only 11,000 southerners—less than 1 percent of the white population—owned more than 50 slaves. However, these powerful planters dominated politics, the courts, and the sheriff's offices in the South.

American Cotton Production

Thousands of whites moved into the interior of South Carolina and Georgia to grow cotton. By 1811, this area was producing 60 million pounds (27 million kg) of cotton a year. Farmers then rushed into Alabama and Mississippi. American cotton production rose from 73,000 bales in 1800 to 335,000 bales in 1820 to more than a million bales in 1840. By 1860, the southern United States grew 60 percent of the world's cotton.

Maria Perkins was a slave in Virginia. In 1852, she wrote to her husband, Richard, that their son, Albert, had been sold and that she would soon be placed on the market:

Dear Husband I write you a letter to let you know of my distress my master has sold Albert to a trader on Monday court day and myself and other child is for sale also. . . .

I want you to tell Dr Hamilton and your master if either will buy me . . . a man by the name of Brady bought Albert and is gone I don't know where. . . . I am quite heartsick nothing more I am and ever will be your kind wife Maria Perkins.

It is not known what happened to Perkins.

THE SECOND MIDDLE PASSAGE

For white Americans, growing cotton meant opportunity. For slaves, it meant misery. Plantation owners in Delaware, Kentucky, Maryland, Virginia, and Tennessee began selling their slaves to people moving to the Deep South. In 1790, planters in Virginia and Maryland owned 56 percent of all American slaves; in 1860, they owned only 15 percent.

Whites uprooted thousands of African Americans from the Chesapeake and Carolina regions and forced them to move southwest. About one out of every four African-American families was broken up by sale. A Georgia slave wrote, "I am Sold to a man by the name of Peterson a trader. My Dear wife for you and my Children my pen cannot Express the griffe I feel to be parted from you all."

Slaveholders often tried to sell their slaves as quietly as possible to avoid trouble with the slaves' families. James Green's owner simply asked his mother if "you will allow Jim to walk down the street with me?" Green recalled, "We walks down the street where the houses grows close together and pretty soon comes the slave market." Green never saw his mother again or even had any chance to say goodbye.

MOVING SLAVES TO THE COTTON STATES

Some owners traveled west with their slaves. In other cases, slave traders purchased slaves to sell at a profit in the new cotton lands. They herded slaves into "pens" in cities like Richmond or Charleston. The slaves were then moved south by train, by boat, or on foot in coffles. One ex-slave remembered, "Dem speculators would put chilluns in a wagon usually pulled by oxen and de older folks was chained or tied together sos dey could not run off."

Sometimes, slaves were sent by boat from the East Coast all the way to New Orleans, Louisiana. This trip took four to six weeks. From the Midwest, steamboats carried slaves as cargo on the Mississippi and Ohio Rivers. This is the root of the expression "to be sold down the river."

Charles Ball was sold away from his family in Maryland. He was chained and forced to wear an iron collar around his neck. Ball said he "longed to die, and escape from the hands of my tormenters; but . . . I could not shake off my chains, nor move a yard without consent of my master."

The slaves would usually be taken to a central market in the Deep South, such as Natchez, Mississippi; Mobile, Alabama; or New Orleans, Louisiana. There, they would be carefully inspected by possible buyers and sold. By 1860, almost 1 million American slaves had been moved from the places of their birth to the booming cotton states. The internal slave trade became one of the biggest businesses in the South.

Fifty Years in Chains

Charles Ball's mother was the slave of a Maryland tobacco planter. The planter died when Ball was four years old, and his family was split up and sold separately. Ball never saw his mother again. In 1805, Ball was sold to a cotton plantation owner in South Carolina while his wife and children remained in Maryland. In 1836, he wrote his autobiography, *Fifty Years in Chains; or, The Life of an American Slave*. The book told how cotton and the cotton gin affected the lives of enslaved African Americans. Ball twice escaped from slavery. No one knows where or when he died.

THE ILLEGAL SLAVE TRADE

Slaves in the United States, unlike in the Caribbean, had enough children to increase their numbers naturally. Because Congress ended the slave trade in 1808, almost all the slaves in the United States in 1860 had been born in America.

An estimated 1,000 African and Caribbean slaves were smuggled into the United States every year in the 53 years between 1808 and the Civil War (1861–1865). Because Americans continued trading in slaves, Congress passed the

Slave Trade Act in 1819. This law allowed the president to use American warships to "seize all vessels navigated under our flag engaged in that [slave] trade." In 1820, Congress made international slave trading an act of piracy punishable by death. That year, five U.S. Navy ships headed for Africa to help put down the illegal slave trade. The American ships stayed on the African coast until 1824.

This woodcut depicts a slave ship being captured off the coast of Cuba in the 1850s.

These American ships joined British ships already there. In 1811, the British had sent warships to patrol the African coast and intercept ships illegally carrying slaves. This British Anti-Slavery Squadron operated off the coast of Africa until

1867. About 2 million Africans were enslaved between 1800 and 1870. The British Anti-Slavery Squadron freed about 150,000 of them.

Denmark outlawed the African slave trade in 1803. Sweden followed in 1813, and Holland in 1814. Most of the new countries carved out of the Spanish Empire in South America also freed their slaves. However, Cuba, Puerto Rico, and Brazil still imported slave laborers from Africa.

On August 23, 1833, Great Britain abolished slavery throughout the British Empire, including the British Caribbean. This Emancipation Act freed more than 700,000 slaves of African ancestry in British colonies.

THE *AMISTAD* INCIDENT

In 1839, Spanish slave traders kidnapped 53 West Africans in present-day Sierra Leone. The slave ship sailed for the Spanish colony of Cuba, where the Africans were transferred to a Cuban ship named the *Amistad.*

Four days after the *Amistad* sailed from Havana, Cuba, the African captives broke free. Led by Sengbe Pieh, who had been renamed Cinque by the slave traders, the slaves took over the ship and killed the captain. The *Amistad* sailed up the east coast of the United States for almost two months until a U.S. Navy ship found it and towed it to Connecticut.

Abolitionists in the United States took up the case of the Africans. Cinque gave a horrifying account of his treatment by the slave traders. He told of the chains, the starvation, the beatings, and the terror of the journey. However, the Spanish government wanted the slaves returned to Cuba.

The *Amistad* case finally went to the U.S. Supreme Court. Antislavery supporters convinced former president John Quincy Adams to argue the case in favor of the Africans. The Africans won the case, and abolitionists helped the 35 who had survived return to Sierra Leone.

THE *CREOLE* INCIDENT

In 1841, a ship named the *Creole* was carrying American-born slaves from Virginia to be sold in New Orleans. The slaves took over the ship, killed one crew member, and forced the captain to sail to the British colony of the Bahamas. There, in accordance with Britain's Emancipation Act of 1833, the British freed the *Creole* slaves.

Some American politicians, newspapers, and citizens said that the British action encouraged mutiny. Abolitionists fought back against this criticism. In 1842, U.S. representative Joshua Giddings of Ohio praised the *Creole* rebels in Congress. He argued that any attempt to reenslave these African Americans would be "unconstitutional and dishonorable." Giddings's speech created an uproar.

In the end, Britain agreed that its officials in the Bahamas had not acted properly. However, the slaves were not returned to the United States. Instead, in 1855, the British paid $110,000 to the American owners of the slaves for their lost "property." The *Creole* incident helped make an issue out of the internal slave trade and slavery itself.

8

The End of the Slave Trade

This engraving from 1832 shows ships of freed slaves coming to Africa.
Some slaves returned to Africa when they gained their freedom, while
others made a life in America.

THE BRITISH FIGHT SLAVERY

Ever since the War of 1812 (1812–1815) against the British, the United States had not allowed the British to search American ships. Southerners still supported slavery, and other Americans felt it would be an insult to the United States for the British to search its ships. Therefore, slave ships from different countries always kept an American flag handy to run up the mast when a British man-of-war came near. This made it impossible for the British Anti-Slavery Squadron to search the slave ships.

Lieutenant Francis Meinell of the British Royal Navy made this 1846 watercolor of slaves on the Spanish ship *Albanoz*. Meinell's ship, the HMS *Albatross*, captured the *Albanoz* and freed the slaves.

One American sailor on an American ship described the problem in his diary. He wrote, "We fired a shot cross [the slaver's] bows, and in a twinkling of an eye, the Stars and Stripes were floating at her peak, no colors have ever been hoisted faster than these were. . . . She thought us to be an Englishman and [if we were], we could not have searched her."

In 1842, right after the *Creole* incident, the British and Americans signed a treaty that created an independent U.S. African Squadron to help put down the slave trade. This U.S. African Squadron, usually about five ships, patrolled the coast of Africa from 1843 to 1860. While the British hunted slavers with some success, Americans contributed very little to the effort. From 1843 to 1857, the U.S. Navy took only 19 slavers. In the same period, the British navy took 600 vessels. Still, the United States would not give permission for the British navy to search suspected slave ships flying the American flag.

THE SLAVE TRADE REFUSES TO DIE

In the 1800s, the British worked hard to close down the slave trade. In 1850, British warships actually sailed into Brazilian ports and fought to seize suspected slavers. However, the slave trade continued as long as there were still markets for slaves in Cuba, Brazil, and the United States. Because the transatlantic slave trade was secret and illegal for most of the 1800s, it is difficult to know how widespread it was. Probably about 2 million Africans were enslaved in the 1800s. Of the 8,000 slaving voyages, about 1,500 ships were seized. About four out of every five slavers avoided capture.

THE SOUTHERN DESIRE
TO REOPEN THE SLAVE TRADE

In the United States, abolitionist attacks on slavery in the 1850s made southerners angry. Southern leaders such as William Yancey of Alabama and Robert Barnwell Rhett of South Carolina responded by supporting the reopening of the transatlantic slave trade. People attending a meeting in Montgomery, Alabama, introduced resolutions stating, "Slavery is right, and that, being right, there can be no wrong in [the slave trade]." When others objected, Yancey replied, "If it is right to buy slaves in Virginia and carry them to New Orleans, why is it not right to buy them in Cuba, Brazil, or Africa and carry them there?" Southern planters at a meeting in Vicksburg, Mississippi, in 1859 voted 40 to 19 that "all laws, State or Federal, prohibiting the African slave trade ought to be repealed."

Henry Eason was a sailor in the U.S. African Squadron. In 1859, he wrote from Africa,

> There is a large barracoon here . . . in which were about 600 young Negroes, of both sexes, who were to be sold for slaves. . . . They can be bought for about $40 per head, in trade and they will fetch from nine to twelve hundred in Cuba.

Some people in the North began the Republican Party in 1854 to prevent the further spread of slavery into the American West. Republicans also opposed the reopening of the slave trade. The Republican Party platform of 1860 stated, "We brand the . . . reopening of the African slave trade, under the cover of our national flag . . . a crime against humanity, and a burning shame to our country and age."

This engraving shows the Republican Convention at which Abraham Lincoln received the nomination for president in Chicago, Illinois, in May 1860.

THE CONSTITUTION OF THE CONFEDERACY

In 1860, the people of the United States elected Republican Abraham Lincoln as president. Eleven Southern states refused to accept the results and decided to secede, or leave the Union. The Southern states declared themselves an independent country, the Confederate States of America, or the Confederacy. They wrote their own constitution, which said that slavery was legal everywhere in their new country.

However, the Confederacy wanted Great Britain to help it remain independent. This meant that the Confederacy could not support the transatlantic slave trade. Therefore, the Southern constitution specifically said, "The importation of negroes of the African race, from any foreign country other than the slaveholding states or territories of the United States of America, is hereby forbidden."

Jefferson Davis was the president of the Confederacy during the Civil War.

Nathaniel Gordon was born in Portland, Maine. He was the son of a respectable seagoing family but became involved in the illegal slave trade and made several slaving journeys to Africa. In 1860, crew members of the USS *Mohican,* one of the ships of the U.S. African Squadron, boarded the *Erie* off the coast of Africa. They found Nathaniel Gordon and 897 slaves, half of them children, in horrible conditions. Gordon claimed he was just a passenger, but the crew testified that Gordon was the captain and had promised them a dollar for each slave they landed in Cuba. He was tried in New York and convicted of international slave trading under the 1820 federal piracy law. President Lincoln refused to pardon him. On February 21, 1862, Gordon was hanged. He was the only North American ever executed in the United States for slave trading.

THE CIVIL WAR

In 1861, the Civil War began between the Northern states and the Southern states. As the war dragged on, President Lincoln and the Republican Party made the end of slavery an important part of their program. They now took steps against slavery that would have been impossible only five years before.

For 60 years, Americans had refused to allow the British to search ships that flew an American flag. In 1862, the Lincoln administration changed the policy. This meant that British ships could finally arrest suspected slavers flying the American flag off the coasts of West Africa and Cuba.

In 1863, President Lincoln's Emancipation Proclamation took effect. This wartime measure issued by the president freed all slaves in the parts of the Confederacy that were still in rebellion. After the war ended in 1865, the Thirteenth Amendment extended this abolition of slavery to the entire United States. Four million slaves—about one-third of the population of the South—were now free.

In February 1862, Nathaniel Gordon became the only North American executed in the United States for slave trading.

AFRICAN AMERICANS IN THE SOUTH AFTER THE CIVIL WAR

The Thirteenth Amendment freed the slaves. Unfortunately, by 1876, they had almost completely lost all their rights as American citizens. For the next 100 years, white people ruled the South. They did not let African Americans vote, run for office, have a fair trial, or even speak freely. Whites passed "Jim Crow laws" that segregated, or separated, blacks and whites in the South. This meant blacks got the worst schools and hospitals. If African Americans protested, they lost their jobs and might even be tortured or killed. This situation did not really begin to change until the 1950s.

The *Henrietta Marie*

In 1972, treasure hunters were exploring the waters off Florida for sunken Spanish treasure ships. About 36 miles (58 km) from Key West, they discovered the underwater wreckage of a ship. On board, divers found almost 100 iron chains. They had found the remains of a slave ship. It was later identified as a British ship, the *Henrietta Marie*.

In 1699, the *Henrietta Marie* left Europe filled with trade goods. On the west coast of Africa, the British exchanged the goods for ivory, gold, and enslaved Africans. The *Henrietta Marie* then sailed to the Caribbean, where the slaves were sold and the ship was loaded with sugar and tobacco to sell in Europe. However, the ship sank in a hurricane shortly after it set sail from Jamaica in 1700. The *Henrietta Marie* is one of the only slave ships ever recovered in the Americas. It is a rare, precious, and unhappy reminder of the slave trade, which had such a huge impact on the people and history of the United States.

However, as bad as things were for African Americans in the South, white southerners never reestablished the worst features of the slave system. Human beings were not bought and sold; husbands were not separated from their wives, or parents from their children. The *Wanderer* probably made the last known landing of slaves in the United States in 1858. The transatlantic slave trade to the United States came to a complete end.

The End of the Slave Trade • 103

Time Line

1444	The first major shipment of African slaves arrives in Portugal.
1538	African slaves first land in northeast Brazil.
1619	John Rolfe reports that "a Dutch man of war that sold us twenty Negars" came to Jamestown, Virginia.
1662	The Virginia legislature declares that slavery is an "inheritable status according to the condition of the mother"—meaning that the children of all enslaved women would also be slaves.
1672	The Royal African Company is founded by the English government in London. It is the only legal slave trading company in England until 1698.
1676	Bacon's Rebellion in Virginia speeds the change from indentured servants to African slaves.
1725	France opens the slave trade to private merchants.
1750	Virginia's slave population of 120,000 makes up almost 40 percent of the colony's population. Indentured servants almost completely disappear. Rhode Island becomes the center of the American slave trade.

1758	The Philadelphia Meeting of Quakers votes to pressure Quaker slave owners to stop participating in the slave trade.
1760	Jamaica's population consists of more than 170,000 African slaves and less than 10,000 whites.
1787	The new U.S. Constitution prohibits the U.S. Congress from passing a law to outlaw the slave trade for 20 years.
1780s	The transatlantic slave trade to North America peaks, with slave traders sending an average of 80,000 Africans every year to be slaves in the United States.
1788	Parliament attempts to regulate slave ships. Thomas Clarkson draws his famous picture of what the Brookes looked like when fully loaded with slaves.
1789	Olaudah Equiano writes *The Interesting Narrative of the Life of Olaudah Equiano,* one of the few views of the slave trade from an African perspective.
1807	Parliament makes it illegal for British ships to carry slaves and for British colonies to import them. Congress prohibits the African slave trade as of January 1, 1808.
1811	The British government sends warships to patrol the African coast and intercept ships illegally carrying slaves.
1814	Holland outlaws the slave trade.
1820	Congress makes international slave trading an act of piracy punishable by death.

1833	Great Britain abolishes slavery throughout the British Empire, including the British Caribbean. This Emancipation Act frees more than 700,000 slaves of African ancestry in British colonies.
1839	The *Amistad* incident takes place.
1858	The *Wanderer* makes what is probably the last known landing of slaves in the United States.
1865	The Thirteenth Amendment to the Constitution abolishes slavery in the entire United States, freeing 4 million slaves, about one-third of the population of the South.
1886	Spain ends slavery in Cuba.
1888	Brazil abolishes slavery.

Glossary

abolitionist   A person who seeks an immediate end to slavery.

barracoon   An enclosure where slaves were kept in temporary confinement.

barter   To trade goods or services without using money.

coffle   A group of chained slaves.

cooper   A barrel maker.

cotton gin   A machine developed in the 1790s to separate the seeds from the fiber of cotton. It led to mass production of cotton and a huge expansion of slavery in the United States.

cowry   A tropical sea mollusk with a shiny or brightly marked shell. The shells were once used as money in some parts of Africa and Asia.

Deep South   Usually refers to the part of the United States that includes Alabama, Arkansas, Florida, Georgia, Louisiana, Mississippi, Texas, and parts of the Carolinas and Tennessee.

emancipation   The act of freeing slaves.

factor   A slave trader who lived at a trading post and sold slaves for a commission.

indenture   A contract that requires a person to work for a master for a certain number of years.

indigo   A dark violet-blue or purple dye that was popular in Europe in the 1700s. Indigo was made from plants grown by slaves in South Carolina and Georgia.

manumit   To free from slavery.

Middle Passage   The voyage of slave ships from Africa to the Caribbean.

mutiny   Rebellion, especially aboard a ship.

Parliament   Great Britain's lawmaking body.

plantation   A large farm that relied on slaves to produce one main crop.

prejudice   An unreasonable bias against or intolerance of others.

racism   Prejudice based on race.

Thirteenth Amendment   An amendment to the U.S. Constitution prohibiting slavery.

West Indies   A group of islands in the Caribbean Sea.

Further Reading

BOOKS

Bailey, Anne. *African Voices of the Atlantic Slave Trade: Beyond the Silence and the Shame.* Boston: Beacon Press, 2004.

Hatt, Christine. *The African-American Slave Trade.* North Mankato, Minn.: Smart Apple Media, 2003.

Monaghan, Tom. *The Slave Trade.* Austin, Tex.: Raintree Steck-Vaughn, 2003.

Thoennes-Keller, Kristin. *The Slave Trade in Early America.* Mankato, Minn.: Capstone Press, 2004.

Worth, Richard. *The Slave Trade in America: Cruel Commerce.* Berkeley Heights, N.J.: Enslow Press, 2004.

WEB SITES

British National Maritime Museum. "Freedom: A KS3 History Resource about Britain and the Transatlantic Slave Trade." URL: http://www.nmm.ac.uk/collections/education/slavery/. Downloaded on June 29, 2005.

Data and Program Library Service (DPLS). "Slave Movement during the Eighteenth and Nineteenth Centuries." URL: http://dpls.dacc.wisc.edu/slavedata/index.html. Downloaded on June 29, 2005.

Mariner's Museum. "Captive Passage: The Transatlantic Slave Trade and the Making of the Americas." URL: http://www.mariner.org/captivepassage/. Downloaded on June 29, 2005.

Public Broadcasting Service (PBS). "The Slave Kingdoms." URL: http://www.pbs.org/wonders/fr_e3.htm. Downloaded on June 29, 2005.

Index